CrossCurrents (ISSN 0011-1953; online ISSN 1939-3881) connects the wisdom of the heart with the life of the mind and the experiences of the body. The journal is operated through its parent organization, the Association for Public Religion and Intellectual Life (APRIL), an interreligious network of academics, activists, artists, and community leaders seeking to engage the many ways religion meets the public. Contributions to the journal exist at the nexus of religion, education, the arts, and social justice. The journal is published quarterly on behalf of the Association for Public Religion and Intellectual Life by the University of North Carolina Press.

The Association for Public Religion and Intellectual Life (formerly ARIL) is a global network of leaders, scholars, and social change agents who explore religious life, engage in intellectual inquiry, and lead ethical action in the world today. Their primary objective, especially through annual summer colloquia and *CrossCurrents*, is to bring together leading voices of our time to advocate for justice and to examine global spiritual and interreligious currents in both historical and contemporary perspectives.

A membership to APRIL includes access to *CrossCurrents* starting with Volume 58, 2008, though our partners at Project MUSE, monthly newsletters, early access to summer colloquium themes, a 40% on UNC Press books, and more. For more information, including membership and subscription rates, visit www.aprilonline.org.

This reissue of *CrossCurrents* was one of four issues published in 2009 as part of Volume 59. For a current masthead visit www.aprilonline.org.

© 2009 Association for Public Religion and Intellectual Life. All rights reserved.

ISBN 978-1-4696-6680-8 (Print)

CROSSCURRENTS

EDITORIAL

100
The Scandal of Particularity
Randi Rashkover

INTRODUCTION TO THE PROJECT

104
Introductory Essay
Christopher M. Leighton

118
Reclaiming Particularity: Reflections on "Reclaiming the Center: A Jewish-Christian Conversation"
Rosann M. Catalano

123
Reflections on the Scandal of Particularity
Andrew Foster Connors

REVELATION

127
Reformed Theology, Revelation, and Particularity: John Calvin and H. Richard Niebuhr
Douglas F. Ottati

144
Jews and Gentiles in the Divine Economy
P. Mark Achtemeier

TEXT AUTHORITY

154
"He Unrolled the Scroll...and He Rolled Up the Scroll and Gave It Back"
Samuel E. Balentine

176
Reverence Despite Rejection: The Paradox of Early Christian Views of Biblical Authority
Adam Gregerman

191
Traveling in Different Directions on the Liturgical Highway
Karen Marie Yust

LAND

197
Land as an Issue in Christian-Jewish Dialogue
John T. Pawlikowski

210
The Place of "Place" in Jewish Tradition
Nina Beth Cardin

PEOPLE

217
Meet the New Paul, Same as the Old Paul: Michael Wychograd, Kendall Soulen, and the New Problem of Supersessionism
William Plevan

POLITICS

229
The Scandal of Particularity: Particularity and the Public Square
Paul D. Hanson

241
Democratic Structures and Democratic Cultures: A "Response" to Paul Hanson and David Novak
Mark Douglas

254
Notes on Contributors

About the Cover: The olive tree is a traditional symbol of Israel and of Jewish-Christian relations. We like the cover photograph by Samantha Veitch because it suggests that this relationship is not static, but is a journey; is not one tree, but many; and leads not in a straight line to a destination already within sight, but beyond the horizons of present understanding. Photograph © Samantha Veitch and iStockphoto.

EDITORIAL

THE SCANDAL OF PARTICULARITY

Knowledge is always about power in one way or another. Politicians, theologians, philosophers, and social theorists have realized this for a long time. We must, Spinoza told us, be wary of ecclesiastical efforts to control belief. Kant distinguished between an ethics rooted in an object we want and a practical knowledge driven by a law "free" from interest. Weber taught us about instrumental knowledge that worked to achieve sought-for ends. Habermas enlightened us to a different sort of knowledge that placed "understanding" over acquisition as its goal but even so, sustained a vision of what constituted "right" knowledge and designated the line drawn to siphon off falsehood. Of course we cannot mention a connection between knowledge and power and not invoke Marx, who taught us that knowledge is not only about acquiring power but about sustaining it as well.

The exposure of power as a factor in knowledge about religion has become a frequently noted phenomenon. The study of religion is not an innocent affair. According to Robert Orsi "[t]he discipline of Religious Studies has always been organized around a distinct and identifiable set of moral values and judgments. The usually unacknowledged centrality of the values in the working life of the discipline has limited the range of human practices, needs and responses that count as religion."[1] Along the same lines, Talal Asad's challenge to Clifford Geertz's definitional approach to religion reminds us that to define is to control. It is to delimit or assert a power over and against the phenomenon one claims to be able to name. No doubt, Geertz saw much of his work as an effort to protect religion from the encroachment of the secular but Geertz's implicit heroism registered as an exercise in intellectual coercion and order-making, here again excising out what remained unruly, contingent, mysterious, and unknowable. Orsi and Asad's insights in-hand, scholars of religion now work to expose what were hidden and sometimes repressed impulses toward containment. This work further illuminated how the effort to contain and control knowledge undermines the very desire for power driving this approach since control is a response to fear or loss—a testimony to powerlessness and the very opposite of authentic power and freedom.

If one applies these considerations to the question of how Jews may know about Christianity and how Christians may know about Judaism, we meet with an extraordinary situation because historically speaking, Jewish–Christian relations did not arise from an effort by either party to retain a status quo. Rather, these relations arose from a dramatically different context of chaos and confusion. The Holocaust left Jews and Christians bereft of power, bereft of the ability to contain and control knowledge not only of the other but of themselves as well. Jewish–Christian Studies emerged within and not outside of the Fackenheimian shadow that demanded a full coming to terms with the suffering of the victims in the Holocaust prior to a retrieval of any piece of Christianity or Judaism. Incapable of naming the event and its players, post-Holocaust Jewish and Christian thought did not lapse into a kenotic undoing. Denuded of power, both traditions sat amidst the confusion of variables, the confusion of positions, the confusion of questions and lost answers. A bombed-out city of broken ideas and shattered foundations, the *Sitz im Leben* of post-Holocaust Jewish–Christian reflection meant a mandated survey of the rubble. Much of what was found was distorted.

We may recall the now famous "Mauriac Foreward"[2] to Eli Wiesel's *Night* with its "What did I say to him? Did I speak of that other Jew, his brother, who may have resembled him—the Crucified, whose Cross has conquered the world?"[3] and the shadow of confusion it cast upon our understanding of that book. We may also recall Richard Rubenstein's interview with Dr. Heinrich Gruber during which Gruber, a man Rubenstein described as "devoted to the work of healing and reconciliation,"[4] nonetheless proclaimed to Rubenstein during the interview that "the problem in Germany is that the Jews have not learned anything from what happened to them...I always tell my Jewish friends that they should not put a hindrance in the way of our fight against anti-Semitism."[5] And when asked, "Was it God's will that Hitler destroyed the Jews?" Gruber (Rubenstein narrates) "arose from his chair and rather dramatically removed a Bible from a bookcase and opened it and read 'for Thy sake are we slaughtered every day' (Psalms 44:22) and continued 'When God desires my death, I give it to him!'"[6]

Still, the undoing of the economy of power has fostered many groundbreaking advances in Jewish and Christian studies. Crucial insights into understanding the Jewish context of Paul's letters, John Howard Yoder's re-telling of Jewish–Christian history and Abraham Joshua Heschel's eulogy for Reinhold Niebuhr, all represent the aftermath of the confusion—the character of knowledge unleashed from the impulses of control. Unentitled to an agenda of containment, Jewish–Christian studies has had to shoulder the obligation to honestly recognize the demise and chaos out of which it developed. It does not have the luxury to excavate easy solutions to difficult questions or apply longstanding definitions of what is and is not the case. It cannot pretend false justifications and more often than not produces less than beautiful and/or comforting analyses.

In the more than fifty years since the end of the Holocaust, there have been many attempts at Jewish–Christian relations. Some of them have been honest, some of them have not. I agreed to participate in the "Scandal of Particularity" because the project was premised upon a problem, the scandal of each tradition's pretense to power and certainty. From its conception, the project sought to engage Jewish and Christian theologians, biblical scholars, clergy and laity in a potentially painful and perplexing review of key elements of each house. Certainly there were times when the conversation lapsed into disingenuous proclamations of how beautiful each religion, is, how great our appreciation for the other, how fortunate we are to share in a Judeo-Christian culture amidst the errors of the secular world. At other times, we did some real work. So many of the papers reasoned from the humility of confusion and so much of the conversation remained honest and searching. This issue is devoted to presenting some of the best of what we found.

–Randi Rashkover

Notes

1. Orsi, Robert, "Snakes Alive: Resituating the Moral in the Study of Religion" in *Women, Gender, Religion*, Elizabeth Anne Castelli, and Rosamond C. Rodman, ed. (New York: Macmillan), 2001, p. 98.
2. Francois Mauriac was a Catholic journalist who encouraged Wiesel's to re-compose his original, Yiddish-written manuscript titled, *And the World Remained Silent* into the much shortened and changed French novel published as *Night*.
3. Francois Mauriac, "Foreward" in Eli Wiesel, "Night" Trans. by Stell Rodway (New York: Bantam Books) 1960, p. x.
4. Rubenstein, Richard L., *After Auschwitz: Radical Theology and Contemporary Judaism* (New York: The Bobbs-Merrill Company, Inc.), 1966, p. 48.
5. Rubenstein, *After Auschwitz*, p. 51.
6. Ibid., p. 53.

INTRODUCTORY ESSAY

Christopher M. Leighton

Interfaith dialogues usually begin with the quest for common ground, and this is where they all too often get stuck. It is exhilarating to discover that people share deep ethical commitments and that they can tap the same wellsprings of human experience. People can share stories and create a shared language that enables them to speak across the ethnic and religious divides and to celebrate their commonalities. Yet the affirmation of common ground all too often fails to get the traction that will move the conversation into uncharted territory. The dialogue yields an exchange of predictable platitudes about the many ways to scale the mountain and the fatuous conviction that they all converge at the top. The conclusion is reached that religious differences are accidental. Our disparate spiritual traditions are mistakenly judged as interchangeable at their core.

Over the past thirty years I have stepped onto the interfaith dance floor and observed countless others march resolutely onto the stage. Most people involved with inter-religious relations have done their share of bumbling and stumbling, and yet many of us have witnessed moments of uncommon grace when radically different partners have brought out the best in one another. In my experience the most searching and transformative engagements have occurred when participants have come together, listened intently to their sacred stories, and explored an array of interpretations that they have not hitherto considered. The surprise is that we often gain a glimpse of the beauty and wisdom of our respective traditions only after we have stepped on some toes, bumped into irreconcilable differences, slipped on unexamined assumptions, and found passionate disagreements can give off warm light as well as a scalding heat.

So the decision of the Institute for Christian & Jewish Studies to collaborate with the Institute for Reformed Theology at Union-PSCE in Richmond, Virginia in a program titled "The Scandal of Particularity" provided an unusual opportunity to embark on a daring theological venture. With the active support and participation of First Presbyterian Church and The Temple: Hebrew Benevolent Congregation of Atlanta, twenty-five Jews and Christians, including scholars, clergy, educators, and lay leaders, embarked on a course of study that would occupy them for the next two years. Each of six two-day meetings revolved around a topic that is foundational to Jewish and Christian self-definitions and yet has historically generated serious misunderstandings between Jews and Christians. We approached each of these sessions by reading sacred texts and classical interpretations from both traditions. Our goals were to identify and develop the intellectual and spiritual resources to probe the depths of our theological differences and to challenge those habits of mind and heart that all too often lock our communities into an adversarial relationship. We invited two visiting scholars to join each colloquy, and we drew upon their special expertise to our frame our conversations. They placed each topic within a broader historical and theological context, highlighted the struggles that have beset our respective communities, and then helped us chart new directions for ongoing exploration. The following summary surveys the questions that the participants examined and hopefully demonstrates the promise of future inquires into our religious particularities.

Session I: Jewish and Christian Understandings of Revelation
Visiting Scholars: Eugene Borowitz (Hebrew Union College) and Douglas Ottati (Davidson College)
November 2006 (in Atlanta)

Jews and Christians are each grounded in revelatory encounters with the divine. In this session we began to explore the relationship between the revelatory experience of Exodus/Sinai within the Jewish tradition and the divine disclosure made known to Christians in the life, death, and resurrection of Jesus. To what degree do the claims that God was manifest in Jesus Christ clash with the fundamental teachings of the Jewish tradition? Is the central theological affirmation of the Jewish tradition, God's Oneness, compromised or even negated by Christian truth claims? In the words of Eugene Borowitz, "when seen through the lens of the Jewish tradition, the Christian claims about the Incarnation are blasphemous." Does that mean the Jewish tradition prompts Jews to dismiss Christian understandings of revelation as unintelligible, theologically scandalous, and at their core idolatrous? Are there any possibilities that Jews may find creative challenges by attending to the ways in which Christians have named God and developed Trinitarian language to express their revelatory experiences?

From a Christian perspective, the story of Jesus is an organic continuation of the revelatory encounters of the Exodus and Sinai. The problematic character of the Christian understanding of its revelation stems from the way that Christians have classically layered their truth claims on top of the Jewish story. Christians have historically insisted that God's promises to Israel are fulfilled in the person of Jesus and the community that formed around him. A theology of replacement, often referred to as "supersessionism," took hold that dismissed "the old covenant" as "obsolete" (see Hebrews 8:13). This negative assessment was reinforced by the exclusivity exemplified in John 14: 6, in which the evangelist portrays Jesus as insisting "I am the Way, the Truth, and the Life. No one comes to the Father except through me."

Although the interchange was more restrained than would prove the case in subsequent meetings, participants were jolted by the discovery of indissoluble differences and by the surprising intuition that the clash of worldviews might illuminate as well as confound our theological routines. We slowly became acclimated at this first session to theological entanglements that stretch back to our communities' beginnings. We found ourselves embroiled in questions that would spill into all of the next five gatherings. Do the accounts of revelations that define Jews and Christians freeze our faith communities into a dangerous rivalry that blinds us to the religious wisdom belonging to the other? Can Jews and Christians learn to think about and interact with one another in ways that recognize and affirm the distinctive ways in which God calls our respective communities into covenant? How might the revelations that have historically set Jews and Christians apart equip us to detect the traces of the divine in the face of the stranger and open us to respond collaboratively to the urgent demands of our broken world?

Session II: The Authority of Scripture
Visiting Scholars: Wendy Zierler (Hebrew Union College) and Samuel Balentine (Union Theological Seminary/PSCE)
March 2007 (in Richmond)

Christians and Jews are sometimes described as people who live within houses of paper. Both communities take their bearings from their distinctive compilations of scriptures, and they discover who they are and how they are to live from these texts. For many Jews the presence of the divine is experienced in the study of their sacred writings. For Christians the Word is discerned in the encounter with the words of their holy writ. Although both communities are aware of the dangers of bibliolatry, each attributes a binding authority to its scriptures and each struggles to preserve scripture's commanding voice in the face of countervailing sensibilities. In this session, participants wrestled with a broad spectrum of problems that emerge when the authority of scriptures is invoked.

The battle for the Bible has a long and twisted history. There have been countless casualties in the tug of war to gain control of biblical interpretation. As evidenced in the one-dimensional parodies by contemporary commentators and pundits, the scriptures are often lambasted as deadly instruments of intolerance wielded by fanatics and blithely accepted by a mindless majority. Beneath the secular censure of biblical and institutional authority reside serious challenges with which both Christians and Jews must grapple.

The group examined one set of questions that revolved around the difficulties of adjudicating between conflicting interpretations of scripture. Over the centuries, biblical texts accumulate multiple layers of meaning, and the same texts can be deployed to justify vastly different ideological agendas. How does a religious community develop new understandings of old texts and in some instances subvert the meaning of the earlier strata of the Bible? More pointedly, how do Christians maintain the sacred status of "Old Testament" when new and different meanings are layered on top? How do Jews honor the binding authority of Tanakh when rabbinic readings are evoked to map out communal paths that diverge from the old understandings? The problem is compounded by each community's ability to generate competing, if not contradictory interpretations. How does the community determine which reading will be normative? Or perhaps the more tellingly question is, who gets to decide the meaning of a text and its appropriate application? Not only do significant contrasts between Christians and Jew come to light in this inquiry, but also the fault lines within Jewish and Christian communities become conspicuous.

The challenge comes into sharp focus when the cultural sensibilities of the ancient world clash with the norms of another era. As tempting as it may be to stone disobedient teenagers, the practice does not mesh with the ethos of subsequent ages. There are strategies of reading that evolved in Jewish and Christian traditions to temper and neutralize biblically warranted customs that became incompatible with community standards. Participants directed careful attention to the patriarchal attitudes that are woven into the scriptures of both Jews and Christians. At issue is the question: How can Jews and Christians develop ways of reading and interpreting their sacred writings that do not render women invisible and speechless? As we know all too well, the fusion of scriptural and patriarchal authority presents both communities with massive difficulties. Yet this dilemma may present unexpected opportunities for creative collaboration among Jews and Christians. In grappling with the following questions, both find themselves on a level playing field up against similarly daunting forces of opposition. Can Christians and Jews repudiate this patriarchal legacy without undercutting the legitimate authority of their scriptural traditions? Does criticism of the cultural attitudes within the scriptures undermine the integrity of the text, relativize the truth claims at the heart of these traditions, and disrupt the vital role that sacred writings have historically played in forming and sustaining religious communities?

Looming in the background of these discussions was the task of dealing with sacred dramas in which the world is divided between "them" and "us." Each of our "master stories" is animated by a struggle in which "the good guys" are pitted against "the bad guys." At critical junctures in our history, we have witnessed the slippage into an apocalyptic worldview in which the battle is reframed as a cosmic struggle in which the forces of light are called upon to destroy the forces of darkness. Given biblically sanctioned precedents, Jews and Christians have good reason to counter those who would use their sacred writings to justify "holy war" and to sanction all manner of violence. Both communities will need to scrutinize the ways in which the authority of scriptures is invoked and take precautions so that the polemical dispositions of their scriptures are not frozen into place.

Session III: Jewish and Christian Understandings of Chosenness and Election
Visiting Scholars: Michael Wyschogrod (University of Houston) and Kendall Soulen (Wesley Theological Seminary)
June 2007 (in Baltimore)

The third colloquy revolved around the questions: What does it mean to be chosen? Does God have "only one blessing" (Genesis 27:38), and does the selection of one people invariably imply the rejection or the inferiority of the other? This concept has set in motion a destabilizing competition over the centuries. Is there something indispensable about the notion of election for Christians and Jews? Many Christians and Jews have argued that God can enter into different covenants with different peoples. Therefore, the notion of chosenness need not devolve into a deadly rivalry. Others call for the abandonment of this category on the grounds that it ineluctably generates distinctions that lead to theological arrogance. Furthermore, in the hands of ideologues, the idea of election has been deployed time and time again to justify imperialistic claims and to sanction territorial and cultural expansion. The rhetoric of Boers in South Africa and the language of a "manifest destiny" in America illustrate the temptations. Given these tendencies, some scholars insist that Jews and Christians alike must abandon their claims to "election" or "chosenness."

In addition, the category of "chosenness" generates a fundamental question about the relationship between Jews and Christians. There are numerous examples within patristic literature in which the Church is presented as the "New Israel." The Church Fathers insisted that the ancient promises of the prophets have come to fruition in the "new covenant," and that there was only one covenant through which people could be in an authentic relationship with God. This view provided the basis for Cyprian's assertion that "outside the Church there is no salvation." In recent decades significant Christian voices have begun to repudiate this "triumphalism." Some insist that God has at least two covenants, one with the Jews and one with the Christians. Others maintain that Jews and Christians belong to the same covenant, although the terms of our participation are distinct. This view leads to the conclusion that Christians and Jews are more deeply connected than any other religious communities. However, is it appropriate for Christians to claim that the people Israel is elastic enough to include both Christians and Jews? How are Jews to assess the Christian claim that the Church is also an essential part of Israel?

The questions of "chosenness" go to the core of our traditions, and participants in the colloquy concluded that there is no way that either Jews or Christians can creatively contend with the challenges of religious pluralism without delving into this inquiry. Until and unless Christians and Jews address the ways in which their identities have been entangled, there is little prospect that either community will fare better with Islam. Given the current political and cultural climate in Europe and the Middle East, the most promising context to pursue this fundamental challenge may be within North America.

Session IV: Jewish and Christian Understandings of Holy Land
Visiting Scholars: Yehezkel Landau (Hartford Theological Seminary) and John Pawlikowski (Catholic Theological Union)
November 2007 (in Richmond)

The fourth session centered on the questions: How did Israel become the Holy Land in the Jewish and Christian traditions, and what religious significance does this place continue to hold for our respective communities? In the wake of the Holocaust, the sociological and political significance of Israel is obvious. Israel serves as an indispensable refuge for Jews, and the bond of this people to this land is often understood as indispensable for Jewish survival. Yet the fusion of land and people also entails religious meanings that many Christians, Muslims, and even secular Jews fail to comprehend. In a profound sense, God is thought to dwell in this territory in a way different than anywhere else on the globe, and many traditional Jews insist that the tradition cannot be as comprehensively embodied elsewhere. Jews have traditionally anchored their hopes and dreams in Israel, and many Jews insist that there is a unique experience of belonging, of being at home in this land. To live in any other place is regarded as exile.

This background set the stage for Yehezkel Landau to assess the challenges of exchanging land for peace and entering into negotiations about settlements on the West Bank. This appraisal requires an evaluation of the biblical and rabbinic traditions that address the issue of sharing the land with other religious communities. How can Israel develop its tradition so that it advances the ideals of justice at the heart of the Jewish heritage in the midst of ongoing warfare? What steps will enable Jews to develop a more robust affirmation of religious pluralism that can take hold within Israel and the Palestinian territories, as well as in North America and Europe? How are Christians to assess the theological status of this land, which continues to have such a potent grip on the hearts and minds of the overwhelming majority of Jews?

Christians also have a deep attachment to the land of Israel, but is the sanctity of this territory the same for both the Christian and Jewish communities? And on what basis do Jews and Christian adjudicate their competing claims on the Land? To be sure, the Holy Land has been a place of pilgrimage for many centuries, and the sacred sites have acquired a sacramental value for many Christians, particularly among the Orthodox and Roman Catholics who have lived continuously in the Middle East. Yet there are strong currents of Christian thought that have spiritualized the significance of Jerusalem and the Holy Land, and these tendencies stem from key passages in the New Testament. In the encounter with the Samaritan woman, Jesus is presented in the Gospel of John as proclaiming, "the hour is coming when you will worship the Father neither on this mountain nor in Jerusalem ... The hour is coming and is now here, when the true worshipers will worship the Father in spirit and truth ... God is spirit, and those who worship him must worship him in spirit and truth" (John 4:20-24). From this perspective, Christians have frequently judged the religious attachment to the land of Israel among many Jews as unintelligible or even idolatrous (in virtue of ascribing infinite value to a finite reality). The condemnations of the State of Israel that have come from Christian communities are not only a response to the plight of the Palestinians, but reflect a deep theological suspicion of the religious meanings attributed to the land by Jews.

This inquiry led to an examination of when criticism of Zionist ideologies and Israeli policies becomes an expression of anti-Semitism. This in turn raised questions that moved to center stage in the final session: What role is appropriate for Christians and Jews to assume in assessing and advocating particular approaches to our country's international policies?

Session V: Jewish and Christian Understandings of Worship
Visiting Scholars: Larry Hoffman (Hebrew Union College) and Martha Moore-Keish (Columbia Theological Seminary)
March 2008 (in Richmond)

During the fourth session, the group examined the ways in which worship shapes the contours of our communities and forms their inner core. The distinctive character of this investigation emerged as participants reckoned with the fact that liturgical practices not only delimit a tradition's corporate identity, they also create perceptions of those who stand outside the community. This inquiry traced some of the ways in which worship has defined the lines of religious demarcation and, in the process, cast the other in a negative light.

The polemical dimensions of Jewish worship were illustrated by a careful examination of the Aleynu poem, which in the thirteenth century became the concluding prayer for liturgical services. This prayer acknowledges God's sovereignty by contrasting the status of Israel with the condition of the other nations.

> We must praise the master of all,
> and render greatness to the creator of the universe,
> Who did not make us like the nations of other lands,
> and did not place us like the families of the earth,
> Who did not make our lot like theirs,
> or our destiny like all of them,
> **For they bow down to nothingness and emptiness,**
> **and pray to a god that will not save** ...

The first stanza celebrates God for giving Israel a distinctive role in the world, and then recapitulates the language of Isaiah by contrasting the idolatrous character of the worship among the nations with its own

INTRODUCTORY ESSAY

prayerful conduct. Although some commentators have noted that these verses need not be read as an assessment of Christianity, the context in the high Middles Ages makes this protestation feeble. According to mystical traditions that assigned a numerical value to the Hebrew letters, the most common name for Jesus has the same numerical value as the Hebrew word for "emptiness." In the mid-sixteenth century, the Roman Catholic Church censored a number of Jewish books, and this verse was excised from the liturgy. Only in the late twentieth century did some Orthodox circles in America and Israel reinstate this prayer. Liberal Jews affirmed the verdict of the censors and have refused to retrieve words that disparaged their neighbors. In the American Reform Movement's 1975 Gates of Prayer, the false gods of the gentiles is turned into the false gods "of our hearts," and thus the words signal an act of self-critical reflection.

The challenges that confront Christians are far more pervasive and troublesome. In this summary I will mention only a few of the more obvious problems with which the churches must contend. The Roman Catholic, the mainline Protestants, and Orthodox Christians all utilize lectionaries that juxtapose readings from "the Old Testament" with lessons from "the New Testament." On numerous occasions, the OT passages profile a promise that is then seen as fulfilled in the person of Jesus. The most celebrated of these texts are recited during the high points of the Christian calendar, namely Advent, Lent, and Easter. The coupling of Old and New Testament readings gives the Bible a seamless quality, which is often reinforced in Christian music (listen to Handel's magisterial work The Messiah or the Advent hymn "O Come, O Come Emmanuel" as salient examples). The logic of the lectionary is so pervasive that many Christians are apt to wonder why Jews do not recognize that their own scriptures lead inexorably to the gospel. Christians are too often oblivious about the ways their liturgical readings and celebrations pile Christological meanings on Israel's story, in the process excising Jews from their own sacred history.

The group brought to light many ways in which "supersessionism" finds powerful expression in Christian worship, and recent newspaper reports have provided confirmation of these deeply engrained habits. The controversy around the reinstated Good Friday prayer in the Tridentine Mass, which calls for the conversion of the Jews, provides an illustrative example. The prayers of World Evangelical Alliance (see the full-page ad in the *New York Times* on March 28, 2008 and subsequent pronouncements from the Berlin conference in September 2008) envision a world in which Jews will be absorbed into the body of Christ. The ethical/theological implications of this hope are obscured by the rhetoric of an all-encompassing love, while this evangelical outreach moves resolutely to fulfill a dream that amounts to spiritual genocide. To develop liturgical practices that honor the ongoing vitality of God's covenant with the Jewish people will demand sustained attention in the years to come and oblige churches to reassess the scope of their evangelical missions.

One of the many dilemmas that increasingly confront Jews and Christians revolves around the issues of interfaith prayer. There are numerous occasions when these communities share a common grief or have cause for civic celebration. Christians and Jews both have a deep spiritual need to put these collective experiences into prayers that bind our communities together and equip us to navigate uncertainty and loss with a renewed sense of hope. Yet the move into interfaith prayer entails a journey into unfamiliar territory, and our religious communities are still in the early stages of developing more inclusive reflexes. Most Christians are accustomed to addressing their prayers to God in Trinitarian and Christological language. Yet this tradition of prayer serves to exclude those who stand outside of the Christian tradition. Indeed, prayers offered in the name of Jesus engender resentments in an interfaith context, alienating participants and undermining the rationale for these gatherings. At issue is the question whether Christians can maintain their authenticity in prayer without explicitly invoking their Trinitarian and Christological convictions. The tradition of Christian prayer is enormously varied, and Christians are being prompted to rediscover a broader and more open language in addressing God. Yet these interfaith events are all too often skewed when the terms of participation require any group to check its most foundational beliefs and practices at the public doorstep. When peoples from different religious traditions come together, should prayer be framed in ways to which everyone can say "Amen"? Or might there be occasions when people pray out their particular traditions while others stand alongside and "participate" at a theological distance? Over the recent decades these tensions have been handled differently, but each interfaith event provides a model of prayer that begs for a more rigorous theological assessment.

Session VI: The Role of Religion in the Public Square
Visiting Scholars: David Novak (University of Toronto) and Paul Hanson (Harvard University)
June 2008 (in Baltimore)

During the final session, participants noted that questions about the role of religion in the public square are frequently assessed in light of the separation of church and state. The rubric for these discussions often distorts the most pressing issues within a democratic polity. Given the plurality of religious voices that vie for our attention and allegiance, the term "church" no longer represents the full spiritual, ethical, and theological spectrum that exerts itself in public debates. A more comprehensive taxonomy is required. More significantly, the ideal of separation sets up a misleading polarity since the lines between "church" and "state" are porous and constantly in the process of renegotiation. The values and practices of a religious community are not confined to the sanctuary, but shape public attitudes and influence government policies. Efforts to purge "the state" of religious suasion are not only futile, but may deprive the society of a critically important agency of change. As Taylor Branch, Pulitzer Prize–winning historian, has observed, religious ideals have inspired and sustained almost every progressive reform movement in America, and politicians who are unable to frame their own political vision in religiously compelling terms rarely evoke the passion and commitment to advance a cause.

While few would deny the enormous power of religious discourse in the political realm, many have legitimate doubts about the appropriate exercise of religious arguments in the public domain. Religious language is rooted in particular communities and grows out of particular traditions, and so the foundational faith commitments are not easily translated into rational explanations that can win universal appeal. In the words of Alasdair MacIntyre, the languages of different religious and philosophical traditions are "incommensurate," and every quest for a universal language of Reason has failed to deliver on its promise. If individuals are anchored within specific communities that are opaque or unintelligible to outsiders, how can a nation establish a common national identity? Does the welter of religious and secular groupings generate a pluribus that overwhelms the sense of an underlying unum? Will religions unleash centrifugal forces that exacerbate the fragmentation of our nation, or can religious communities develop new models of understanding, welcoming the stranger and cultivating our receptivity to the human family in all its multiplicity?

The entanglements of "church and state" make a clean separation impossible, and yet the mixture of the two can sometimes make a combustible combination. A democracy always runs the risk of privileging the majority religion and encroaching on the liberties of minorities. In his volume Religious Outsiders and the Making of Americans, R. Laurence Moore observed that the United States did not establish the freedoms so essential to divergent religious communities because American Christians espoused theological worldviews compatible with the realities of religious pluralism. Rather, the jumble of religious loyalties made it difficult for any one denomination to superimpose its view on others or to exercise its authority to mute dissenting positions. The challenge remains for our religious traditions to catch up with the lived reality of most Americans. The task is for believers who position themselves as the majority to discover the blessings that come from our religious diversity and the benefits that stem from our political configuration. As Bishop Krister Stendahl, of blessed memory, frequently reminded us, our religious communities must realize that "in God's eyes we are all minorities."

I am frequently struck by a counter-intuitive discovery that Jews and Christians frequently make in the process of serious and sustained study: Dialogue partners often find their voice in the encounter with one another. Rather than meld into an amorphous mix, the distinctive character of each tradition comes into sharper focus. Not only do the beliefs and practices that give each community its particular texture emerge from the interplay, but the underlying religious alignments and unspoken assumptions of each tradition rise to the surface. New interfaith encounters between peoples who come from other religious traditions will generate fresh insights into their own scandalous particularities. Yet the surprising insights that emerge from disciplined inquiries among Christians and Jews offer instructive clues, if not a model for other interfaith partnerships.

The significance of these educational adventures is rarely woven into the fabric of congregational life, and graduates of our colleges and universities seldom realize the promise of interfaith study in the course of their educations. Which is to say that our schools, seminaries, churches, synagogues, mosques, temples and ashrams are not doing an adequate job of showing us how to live within a religiously plural world, and this failure redounds to the detriment of the society at large. If Jews, Christians, Muslims, Hindus and Buddhists have distinctive contributions to make to the public square, they will first need to develop and hone their insights through rough and tumble exchanges with one another.

Our country and our world stand face to face with new ethical and spiritual quandaries, and our responses to these conundrums will in large measure determine the substance and character of our society. When we enter the domain of bio-ethics and contend with technological breakthroughs (stem-cell research and genetic engineering), when we confront our obligations as stewards of God's creation and contemplate a variety of environmental guidelines and policies, when we are called to assess the distribution of limited resources and to weigh our duties to those who are vulnerable and desperately in need, we confront profound religious questions that redound powerfully on the larger polity. How will the judgments of one tradition be brought to bear on the views of others? Can religious communities temper their absolutist tendencies and translate their particular insights in ways that are morally persuasive to the larger public?

Next Steps

Each conversation left in its wake a plethora of sacred fragments, and we look forward to many exchanges in the years to come, when we can circle back to reassemble the pieces of the puzzle and discover surprising configurations. Given the ongoing clashes that are currently fueled by conflicting religious and ethnic alignments, the need for new educational models will increase. The experiments will need to prove the transformational power of interfaith encounters and demonstrate the benefits for the just and democratic ordering of our society. With its partners in Atlanta, Richmond, and Baltimore, the Institute for Christian & Jewish Studies will design and develop new resources to inspire other churches, synagogues, colleges, and seminaries to embark on the adventure. The inquiries that are featured in this issue of CrossCurrents hopefully underscore the imperative and substantiate the promise.

RECLAIMING PARTICULARITY
Reflections on "Reclaiming the Center:
A Jewish-Christian Conversation"

Rosann M. Catalano

eclaiming the Center: A Jewish–Christian Conversation is a multiphase project of the Institute for Christian & Jewish Studies in Baltimore, MD. The second phase of the project, entitled "The Scandal of Particularity," was a series of colloquia that the ICJS pursued in partnership with Union Theological Seminary/Presbyterian School for Christian Education in Richmond, VA.

Comprised of six two-and-one-half day sessions that took place over the course of two and one-half years, "The Scandal of Particularity" brought together nineteen participants, with equal numbers of Jews and Christians, academics and educators, clergy and lay leaders. Additionally, three ICJS scholars, two scholars from Union/PSCE, and two visiting scholars for each session joined the group of nineteen who met for six sessions over the life of the project.

The goal of the project was to create a community of learners whose focus was the exploration of six theological categories that (1) are foundational to the religious self-identity of each tradition, (2) are shared by both traditions, (3) are understood differently by each tradition, and (4) are oftentimes the source of deep misunderstanding. The topics were The Particularity of Revelation; The Authority of the Text; The People Israel, The People of God (chosenness); The Particularity of Place (land and the embodiment of the divine); Worship and the Particularity of the Other; and Particularity and the Public Square (the role of religion in democracy).

What follows is a series of reflections and observations that I found to have lasting value and long-term consequences for the future of the Jewish–Christian conversation.

The emphasis on diversity
There were benefits to the multilayered diversity of the group's composition that emerged over time.

a. Having women, men, Jews, Christians, academics, clergy, educators, seminarians, and lay leaders around the table made for a diverse conversation even within faith-alike groups. Participants were able to experience real difference *within* traditions, as well as *between* traditions. That proved to be extremely instructive precisely because it unseated one of the most frequent—and dangerous—misunderstandings of the other tradition: that "they" are a monolithic community of believers who all worship the same way and believe the same things, while "we" are a community that is broadly diverse!

b. A second benefit of the group's multilayered diversity proved to be the biggest discovery for a number of participants, namely, that in any given discussion, they oftentimes held more in common with some of their Jewish or Christian counterparts than they did with some in their own tradition. For some more than others, that was both a discovery and a surprise.

The emphasis on particularity
In the early days of the dialogue, an unspoken rule seemed to govern the discourse.

a. Topics on the table for discussion would be limited to those that had the potential to reveal what the two traditions held in common. The goal, it seemed, was to steer clear of any and all conversation that might disclose any deep divisions or disagreements. In brief, the early days might best be characterized as an exercise in "making nice," understandable given the tragic history that Jews and Christians shared.

b. "The Scandal of Particularity" set for itself a quite different goal: to inhabit that dialogic space that most clearly reveals what makes each tradition distinct. It is indeed a sign of the maturity of the dialogue that the exploration of difference turned out to be the single greatest catalyst for learning about and coming to understand the other. Perhaps the greatest breakthrough of this project, at least in terms of pedagogy, was that the emphasis on discovering what makes each tradition unique yielded far greater and more lasting learning than did the emphasis on learning what both communities hold in common.

The "practice of particularity"

The emphasis on learning and discussion that intentionally focused not on what Jews and Christians share, but rather on what makes them distinct and particular, especially in the ways in which each community interprets and makes meaning out of life's events and experiences, resulted in two separate but related by-products that, I believe, have lasting value for the future of the dialogue. The first is what I call the discipline of "practicing particularity"; the second, the awareness that each participant is simultaneously teacher and learner.

a. The "practice of particularity" is a learned behavior that rests upon the notion that the goal of interfaith dialogue is twofold: (1) to articulate as clearly as possible what most essentially and clearly identifies us religiously and (2) to learn from the other what most essentially and clearly identifies them religiously. The art of doing both successfully requires that participants be quite intentional as regards the manner in which they frame their conversation. The "practice of particularity" entails speaking in declarative sentences when speaking of one's own tradition, and speaking in interrogative sentences when speaking of the other's tradition. What became clear in the course of the project's life is that this twofold way of speaking keeps in check two tendencies that are detrimental to genuine dialogue and learning: (1) the tendency to speak only in generalities so as not to offend the other, the result of which is that little, if any, light is shed on what makes us who we most truly are, and (2) the tendency to speak *for* the other rather than to allow the other to speak for him/herself.

b. The second by-product of "practicing particularity" was the realization that all participants were simultaneously learners and teachers. They are teachers of the other and of their own tradition when they speak declaratively about the distinctive ways of thinking, appropriating reality, and making meaning that are unique to their community; and they are learners when they engage the other tradition interrogatively, when they "make room" for the other to speak declaratively for and about him/herself. An illustration of this "practice" is exemplified in the formulation of the two most common questions asked and answered: (1) What do I most want known about my own tradition? (2) What do I most want to know about the other's tradition? In short, the simultaneity of learner/teacher helped create a level playing field where all members of the conversation inhabit both roles.

Some ingredients for success
Additional ingredients that contributed to the success of the project ought to be noted for future meetings. In no particular order, but of equal value, are the following:
a. Project participants were all deeply committed to and observant members of their own tradition.
b. Participants were remarkably open to the most profound—and frightening—aspects of *true* dialogue, namely,
  i. that their ideas about the other and the religion of the other might be overturned in the process of studying with, listening to, and learning from them;
  ii. that some aspects of their own tradition, especially what it teaches about the other, might come into conflict with what they come to learn about and from the other.
c. Over time, participants became increasingly aware that *together* they were engaged in what they deemed to be important work, a realization that created a profound sense of ownership for the project and responsibility to one another for the success of the project.
d. Three components of the meeting structure also contributed to the success of the project.
  i. Spreading the meetings out over thirty months gave participants time and opportunity to think about what they had learned, digest the learning, formulate questions that they brought to the next session, and incorporate what they wanted into their own thinking.
  ii. Having each session meet over two and one-half days was, I think, crucial for the success of the project because studying together, sharing meals, and enjoying free time together helped create a real community of learners who became friends, a special kind of magic that cannot happen in a two-hour block of time meeting over a number of weeks.

iii. Multiple opportunities for small group text study with the same people created a sense of intimacy and safety. These sessions proved to be enormously important to the creation of community.

Finally, my participation in "The Scandal of Particularity" was again a reminder of what is possible when religiously committed people of good will and open minds sit around the table and study together, and in the process, come to experience the magic that can occur only when theological humility meets a willingness to listen and learn, when the knowledge that *all* human knowing is partial meets a genuine desire to learn, and when confidence that the God of the universe seeks out each of us and all of us, each in our own way, to contribute to repairing the brokenness of the world.

REFLECTIONS ON THE SCANDAL OF PARTICULARITY

Andrew Foster Connors

Serving as a the pastor of a self-described "progressive" Presbyterian Church with deep connections in the Jewish community I was somewhat skeptical about what I, and more importantly, the community of Christians I serve might take away from the Scandal of Particularity. Many Christians in my congregation are already painfully aware of the legacy of anti-Semitism with the Church. In fact, the awareness of our history, at times, has made many within our community reluctant to embrace core claims of our faith—claims related to Jesus, biblical authority, and the Church.

Perhaps, too, this skepticism was nurtured in interfaith conversations shared among self-described "progressive" Jews, Christians, and Muslims where the tenor of the conversation often led to the false and unsatisfying conclusion that we are "all the same," or we are all "paths leading to the same one truth"—a conclusion that obliterated rather than respected the claims of "the other."

My skepticism soon abated as new colleagues, many well-versed in Jewish–Christian dialogues, took the reverse approach. Instead of looking for those places where our faith convictions overlap, we went directly to conversations about difference. What was shared was not always a common approach, or common faith conviction, but rather a desire to understand our differences, to grapple with ways those differences have led to harm in the past, and bring fresh, imaginative approaches to ways in which our differences might lead not to harm but to healing, and a deepening of our respective traditions.

Given the fact that Christianity emerged from Judaism, claims a core text from Judaism, worships the God of Israel, and claims that a Torah-observant Jew was in fact the Messiah, one would think that Christians would know a great deal about Jews and Judaism. Alas, this is not the case. Those of us in the preaching profession, in particular, regularly extrapolate erroneous perspectives on today's Jews and Judaism from New Testament readings born in the conflict between an emergent church and changing synagogue. Most Christians—seminary trained or not—have little idea what Jews mean when they refer to the "oral law" and the "written law," or "the rabbis," or "Halakah."

If the Scandal of Particularity had achieved nothing other than the re-education of several pastors, then it would be a success. I walk away from the Scandal with a rich appreciation for the history of interpretative thought, a greater understanding of the sources and norms that inform Judaism as well as the ways in which those sources and norms continue to be contested. I have a renewed understanding of the diversity of ways in which "chosenness," or election, is interpreted and functional for Jews and Judaism, as well as the threats of assimilation which confront Jews who are seeking to hold onto the center. And I have an incomplete, yet emerging understanding of the importance of land and the ways in which Christian ignorance in this area can run counter to mutually held hopes for peace.

The concept of election, is one area worth extended reflection since it has ongoing significance for Judaism and for Christian theology, particular my own Reformed understanding of the Church. In one fruitful conversation, I was privileged to hear Michael Wyschogrod argue against the liberal notion that the people Israel are elected based on ethical criteria. Rather, God's election is a carnal election—"in the flesh"; the election of a people descended from the seed of Abraham. This provocative view led to a spirited debate among the Jews present about just what it means to be Jewish. The dispute was an important reminder that foundational issues within each of our faiths are not static, but highly and repeatedly contested.

As provocative and challenging as Wyschogrod's argument was for the Jews in the room, it opened a new way of understanding my own faith's struggle to define itself in relationship to Judaism. Using Pauline texts, Wyschogrod argues that, according to Paul, the Christ event had a different significance for Gentiles than for Jews. For gentiles, the Christ event opened the door to a kind of "associate membership" for gentiles—a way for gentiles to worship the one God of Israel. That is, gentiles who were willing to obey the Noachide Laws and who had faith in Jesus as the Messiah became part of the house of Israel. For Jews who followed Jesus as Messiah, the Christ event did not abrogate the law, but rather made certain that God's mercy was sure when they failed in their earnest attempts to uphold it completely.

The implications of such a reading are challenging for both Jewish and Christian communities. To Christians, Wyschogrod argues that if Paul is still authoritative then Jews who embrace Christ must be persuaded *by the church* to maintain their identity by, among other things, rejecting intermarriage and continuing to maintain Torah as *Jewish* Christians. To Jews, Wyschogrod argues that Jews must take seriously whether or not there is room in the synagogue for "Noachide converts"—that is, gentiles who wish to become part of Jewish people, taking seriously the Noachide Laws as a kind of "Torah" for gentiles.[1]

I cannot say I am fully converted (!) to Wyschogrod's way of thinking, but I am at once challenged and invigorated by his new reading of ancient texts. I find it wonderfully ironic and instructive than an orthodox Jew is one who has opened my understanding and appreciation Paul—a primary architect of my own faith. Yet on reflection, my serendipitous surprise feels more like brutal ignorance for never before imagining that an observant Jew might better be able to understand the Pauline perspective. These kinds of awakenings are less and less surprising to me the more I spend time in study with my Jewish sisters and brothers.

I come away from the Scandal of Particularity with a number of unanswered, yet focused questions. Among them: How do diverse ways of understanding election among Jews and Christians create opportunities for new relationship and/or threats to each other? Is a new Jewish privileging (some might say rediscovery) of the written Torah helpful for conversations with Protestant Christians? How widely is this move observed/accepted among religious Jews? Related, how do Christians and Jews relate to one another at a time when sources and norms and institutions of authority are contested? In relationship to the question of land—what is Jesus' view of land? What are the views of the communities that produced the gospels in relationship to land? Is land absent from their programs or integral to it? How should Christians relate to the question/theology of land and election in our own core convictions? Is there space within Judaism for gentile believers in the God of Israel or are Christians part of an undifferentiated mass of non-Jews? What would such a space look like?

As a pastor I also come away with a host of practical questions, many of which remain unanswered. These include, how can Christians preach the Old Testament in a way that does not lead to an unstated, yet operative supersessionism? How do Christians preach New Testament texts which emerged out of times of conflict and tension in a way that both preserves the narrative power of text and does not give rise to new anti-Semitism? How should Christians relate to interfaith marriage—not simply the theological approach, but the pastoral approach to families already present in our congregations? Should pastors and rabbis form a common approach? What is happening in interfaith prayer? Is interfaith prayer the highest expression of mutual respect, or a well-intentioned way of obliterating our particularities and therefore endangering each other? Is study the only way to come together? the best way? for Jews? for Christians?

I come away with a number of questions, but with a new confidence and hope that these questions are approachable, not simply through autonomous scholarship but with colleagues who I need to know in order to deepen my own faith. I come away with a deep sense of gratitude for my own Christian faith, and for the faith of my Jewish brothers and sisters. Ultimately, I return to the pulpit with a conviction that the core claims of my faith need not be harmful to Jews, especially when those core claims are made transparent in dialogue and study with colleagues who are invited to question, illuminate, and interpret them. In fact, I believe that it is this kind of dialogue that results in Jews who are better Jews and Christians who are better Christians because of each other.

Note
1. I highly recommend Michael Wyschogrod's book, *Abraham's Promise: Judaism and Jewish-Christian Relations* (Grand Rapids, MI: Eerdmans, 2004) particularly the chapter entitled, "Paul, Jews, and Gentiles." The introduction by R. Kendall Soulen also should not be missed.

REFORMED THEOLOGY, REVELATION, AND PARTICULARITY
John Calvin and H. Richard Niebuhr

Douglas F. Ottati

Reformed Christianity, as I shall soon have reason to emphasize, is but one of many particular Christian sub-traditions. Thus, when we investigate how Reformed theologians understand a theme such as revelation and particularity, we are in little danger of emerging with a statement of how Christian theologians at large or in general understand it. We can emerge, at best, with an understanding of how persons and groups within this particular Christian sub-tradition understand it. Moreover, we should also note that there have been significant disagreements over revelation even within the specific strand of Christian tradition known as Reformed. The American fundamentalist–modernist controversy, for example, was partly a conflict over how to understand biblical revelation in relation to other sources of insight. During the twentieth century in Europe, Karl Barth complained that Emil Brunner embraced a theology of compromise which threatened the independence of revelation from alien sources of insight.[1]

My purpose here, accordingly, is not to identify THE Reformed understanding of revelation and particularity, but only to provoke reflection on this theme by indicating how some Reformed theologians have understood it. Specifically, I will review John Calvin on revelation and the covenant of grace and H. Richard Niebuhr on revelation and the purpose of the church. That is, I will review two related but different expressions of the Reformed theological tradition drawn from two different places and times. In each instance, I will try to show how an understanding of revelation and, indeed, of the historically particular revelation of God in Jesus Christ relates to other rather expansive themes and ideas—at least some of which touch upon Reformed theological views of Judaism as well as of other religions.

Reformed Christianity

Let me begin by observing that there is no generic Christianity, just as there is no generic Hinduism or Islam. Instead, there are different Christian churches and strands, each with its own distinctive history, institutional forms, doctrines, services of worship, practices, etc. There are Roman Catholic, Greek Orthodox (and Armenian Orthodox), and Protestants. Among Protestants, moreover, there are further subdivisions: Lutherans, Reformed, Mennonites, Anglicans, Baptists, Methodists, (later on) Pentecostals, and more.[2]

There are important and broad commonalities among these groups. All preach the gospel of Jesus Christ. Many share elements of the so-called ecumenical creeds (the Nicene Creed and the Apostles' Creed). But it is also true that the several ecclesial traditions often interpret the Gospel somewhat differently, and that, to a degree, plurality is already a feature of the New Testament itself with its four gospels. Moreover, there is no single *text* of the creed that is affirmed by all. Different churches accord the creeds different measures of authority, and some churches are explicitly non-creedal, e.g., the United Church of Christ and many Baptist churches.

Major ecclesial strands may be regarded as somewhat distinctive *traditions* of understanding the Gospel and Christian faithfulness that, in turn, frame somewhat different approaches to the understanding and interpretation of the Bible. Thus, among Mennonites and other Protestant groups that trace their heritage to the so-called "left wing" of the Reformation of the sixteenth century (and many of which are historically pacifist), there is an emphasis on the reign of Christ in opposition to fallen earthly powers. The baseline for faithful living among these groups is following Jesus as a radical and rigorous disciple. Revelation centers on Jesus and his teaching, and this accords with a sharp focus on the portraits of Jesus in the synoptic gospels. By contrast, Lutherans often emphasize a distinction between law and gospel (or grace). This emphasis is joined with the idea of justification by faith as well as the idea that faith is active in love. These ideas correlate with a suspicion of "legalism" and imitation of Jesus in ethics, and with a stress on certain Pauline epistles (perhaps most notably Galatians).

Reformed churches tend to focus on our faithful response to God's sovereign and universal reign and, then, within the rather broad sweep of this image, they emphasize free grace but also sanctification and law. Revelation, then, has to do with knowledge of God and God's reign (a sovereign rule that includes a positive place for civil government and political powers) and our place within it. This emphasis accords with a comparatively high regard for the Old Testament, since Reformed Christians understand the divine governance to be illumined throughout the scriptures. Practically speaking, it also supports a *worldly impetus*; since no place and no area of life lies beyond God's universal governance, we are called to respond faithfully to God in all places and in all areas of life or in the midst of things. This impetus, in turn, coheres with a stress on our calling to participate faithfully (or both constructively and critically) in the activities and institutions of society, e.g., family, commerce, law, and government. (Now you know why there are so many Presbyterian lawyers and judges.) By contrast, Protestant ecclesial traditions that emphasize radical discipleship sometimes shun government service, civil courts, and the military.

For Reformed Christianity, then, emphasis falls on a life oriented toward God and God's encompassing reign. Theology is essentially a practical wisdom that helps persons to lead faithful lives, or to orient themselves appropriately in relation to God and others. It is a reflective enterprise that tries to help us envision God, the world, and ourselves in relation.

John Calvin's understanding of theology

How this is so will become clearer if we recall the first sentence of John Calvin's *Institutes of the Christian Religion*. "Nearly all the wisdom we possess, that is to say true and sound wisdom, consists of two parts: the knowledge of God and of ourselves."[3] Knowledge of God and of ourselves is a wisdom or existential knowledge that we *are* (not our own but) in relation to the one Creator and Governor, the source and fountain of every good. For Calvin, human life is appropriately oriented when, out of gratitude for the goodness and many gifts of the one God on whom we and all other creatures depend, we, in turn, live lives of faithfulness and praise. Thus, knowledge of God and God's benevolence toward us is the baseline in Calvin's theology for both piety and faith.[4] His fundamental claim was that, in order to get human life right, we need to understand ourselves rightly in relation to God and, in order to get God right, we need to understand God rightly in relation to ourselves. The focus, then, is on a *relation* or an encounter that discloses God's goodness and therefore yields important wisdom. Indeed, Calvin supported what he called a "Christian philosophy" or what we might even term a "Christian humanism."[5] He thought highly of the Socratic dictum, "Know thyself," although he would have amended it to read, "Know God, know thyself."

For Calvin, then, theological knowledge or wisdom was an essentially practical matter that has to do with how human life is to be oriented. Like many other (and later) Reformed theologians, including the writers of The Westminster Confession of Faith, he believed that the purpose of human life is to know and to glorify God. Thus, the last sentence of his *Institutes* (which appears in capital letters): "GOD BE PRAISED."[6]

If we ask how we are to praise God, the basic answer is that we are to respond faithfully to the divine governance in all areas of life, or in the push and shove of our many interactions with objects, others, situations, and realities. But to do this, we need some vision of the many objects, others, situations, and realities in relation to God. We need to picture them in the context of the divine governance. Thus, for example, if I am to interact with my daughter, the Pentagon, and the natural environment in a manner that is also faithfully responsive to God, I need to fashion an accurate vision or picture of how I am related to God as well as how my daughter, the Pentagon, and the Earth's ecology are related to God. That is, I need a theology based on true knowledge of God and ourselves.

Calvin on revelation

This true knowledge of God of God and God's benevolence, this encounter with the great and good God, was for Calvin the substance of revelation. He believed that a seed of it is sown in all persons, and that this is especially apparent in human conscience and moral sensibility. In addition, "knowledge of God shines forth in the fashioning of the universe and the continuing government of it," and there are "innumerable evidences of both in heaven and on earth that declare God's wisdom."[7] The world, in fact, is the theatre of God's glory.[8]

Unfortunately, said Calvin, people turn ungratefully away from and against God. They confuse Creator with creatures and fashion God according to their own whim. They imagine God according to their own liking (a source of idolatry), and they fail to know God as the faithful fountain of all good. So, the seed of religion in persons is dimmed and the manifestation of God in "the mirror of his own works" is obscured by human superstition, error, and sin.[9] In this dimmed and obscuring condition then, we are unable to come to true knowledge of God and ourselves apart from revelation of Jesus Christ, the Son. Here, we finally come to know God and ourselves accurately and truly. And, in the course of Calvin's theology, this means that we come to know ourselves as good creatures, as corrupted sinners, and as beneficiaries of renewing grace in relation to the good God who creates, judges, and redeems.

Calvin claimed that this knowledge has been written down in scripture and, in Book Four of his *Institutes*, he commented on the question of revelation and scripture in a manner that clarifies their relationship. Calvin said that only "the Son" sees "the Father." But the Son is not simply identical with the man Jesus of Nazareth. The Son is God's "sole wisdom, light and truth" who is active in the fashioning of the world and communicating with people. Thus, it was by the Son, Calvin said, that Adam, Noah, Abraham, Isaac, and others received "heavenly teaching." Subsequently, then, when God raised up a more visible form of religious community, God also "willed to have his Word set down and sealed in writing, that his priests might seek from it what to teach the people."[10] The law or the Torah was therefore published. Then, in due time, also by means of the Son or God's wisdom, new oracles were added through the prophets. These too were committed to writing in order to reveal a clearer doctrine, teach weak consciences, and so forth. Later still, the Word (Son or wisdom of God) became flesh in Jesus Christ, taught and was heard, and the apostles were charged to commit these teachings to writing.[11]

This entire collection of writings (the Law, the Prophets, and the New Testament) is the Word of God *written* and, according to Calvin, the heavenly teaching expressed in them was also received earlier by some in an unwritten form. The collection of writings came to be under the auspices, as it were, of the Son or wisdom of God, and it remains the standard for true knowledge of God and ourselves. It furnishes "spectacles" that correct our dimmed and skewed vision of God, the word, and ourselves.[12] And, indeed, a true knowledge of God and ourselves in relation to God requires that we be reoriented and turned. It puts us, as it were, in our proper place by telling us that we are not the central point of all things, but participants in a rich and varied creation governed by God, and that we depend on the divine fountain of goodness for both life and new life.

Now, all of this—scripture, the sense of the divine in humans, and the manifestation of God and God's wisdom in the world—needs to be interpreted and made use of if we are to live appropriately in relation to God, or to praise God in the midst of our interactions with objects and others. This need signals a role for a *theological tradition*. Calvin therefore claimed that apostles, prophets, evangelists, pastors, ministers, and teachers have been appointed to build up the church by preaching and teaching. They are interpreters who educate persons in the church by teaching doctrine and overseeing public worship, so much so that the church may be likened to a school.[13] Thus, although the Protestant Reformer recognized that church councils are subject to human failings, he also maintained that they may help us to understand God and ourselves.[14]

To be sure, for Calvin and his followers, such tradition was subordinate to scripture and therefore subject to criticism in the light of scripture. Even so, it is arguable that we never have scripture apart from interpretation or apart from tradition of some sort, which is why Heinrich Bullinger's Second Helvetic Confession follows its first chapter on scripture with one on the interpretation of scripture.[15] Moreover, as the Scots Confession of 1560 affirmed, where tradition accords with scripture, it has an important use or function. We receive tradition critically, but we also receive it with respect because, by their teachings, confessions, and statements, those who participate in the church offer "a public confession of their faith to generations following."[16] Or, as we might say, by means of tradition, those who participate in the church furnish interpretations of revelation; they make use of the knowledge of God and ourselves it proffers in order to envision in relation to God themselves and the many objects and others with which they interact in their own place and time. Tradition, in this sense, is theology; it offers an interpretation of things in relation to God, and we are able to enter into conversations with past theologies and testimonies. Receiving them with critical respect, we may make use of them as *we* attempt to envision in relation to God ourselves and the many objects and others with which *we* interact today, e.g., my daughter, the Pentagon, the Earth's planetary ecology. That is, we enter into conversation with our received theological tradition as we attempt to do in our time and place what past Christian communities did in theirs, or as we attempt to formulate and construct our own theological vision in our own place and time.

The covenant of grace

Consider now an important and rather expansive theme in Calvin's theology. There is one covenant of grace, founded on Christ alone, but this covenant includes figures such as Adam and Noah who antedate Judaism, Jewish patriarchs and prophets, New Testament apostles, and later followers of Jesus.[17] Accordingly, Calvin regarded baptism in close association with election, and said that it parallels circumcision as an entrance into the covenant community. Indeed, while discussing this sacrament, Calvin claimed "the gifts and the calling of God are without repentance" (Romans 11:29, Vulgate), and that the blessing of the covenant God made with the Jews "still rests among them."[18]

The basic point goes to the heart of Calvin's theology of grace and election. "The covenant made with all the patriarchs is so much like ours in substance and reality that the two are actually one and the same."[19] God's covenant with the Jews, then, is a function of election by grace and it communicates the divine goodness or benevolence. God chooses Israel freely and bestows God's blessing as a gift; not as a consequence of Israel's special merit and not on condition of its special virtue. This, in fact, is how Calvin understood Leviticus 26:12, "I will be your God and you shall be my people." Again, he noted, the "life energy in God's Word…quickens the souls of all to whom God grants participation in it," and "Adam, Abel, Noah, Abraham, and the other patriarchs" enjoyed "a real participation in God."[20] Following Paul, then, Calvin claimed that, in Christ, the Gentiles are, as it were, engrafted onto this same covenant.

The basis for the blessing and salvation of both Jew and Gentile is therefore the same, namely, the free, gracious and irrevocable election, gift and calling of God. Others may argue that this free gift and calling somehow has been withdrawn from the Jews. Theologically and systematically speaking, however, this option was not really available to Calvin. For, in his terms, to claim that the covenant with the Jews is either superseded or withdrawn would be to say that the free grace and election of God are not without repentance but are indeed revocable. But this line of thinking undercuts all human reliance on God's free goodness and so it imperils the free election of all, both Gentile and Jew.

Calvin understood the law to comprise not only the Ten Commandments "but the form of religion handed down by God through Moses" and, as one might expect, he had a comparatively positive appreciation for it.[21] Indeed, he believed that opposition between law and gospel should not be exaggerated, that grace is a feature of the law, that the gospel does not abrogate the law, and that believers in Christ have need of the law in order to lead faithful and sanctified lives. The gospel, he insisted, confirms the law and it does not "bring forward a different way of salvation."[22] Differences between the law and the gospel are attributable to the fact that there are two dispensations of the same covenant of grace. However, these differences pertain to matters of administration and *not* substance. Thus, for example, in Calvin's view, the New Testament is clearer and the Old Testament more obscure. The New Testament is given to all nations (and is therefore universal), whereas the Old Testament is given to one particular nation. The reason these differences exist is that God, ever the consummate pedagogue, accommodated different forms of expression to different ages.[23]

A similar understanding of the one covenant of grace lay behind Chapters 4 and 5 of the Scots Confession of 1560, which treat the revelation of God's promise as well as the church *before* Chapter 6 on "The Incarnation of Christ Jesus." As far as the writers of this confession were concerned, then, the promise was received "by all the faithful from Adam to Noah, from Noah to Abraham, from Abraham to David, and so onwards to" Christ. Moreover, God has called all the faithful since Adam into the true "Kirk" (Scottish dialect for church).[24] That is, in this context, the true church cannot simply be equated with visible Christianity.

To summarize, Calvin claimed that the particular revelation in Jesus Christ affords us knowledge of God (the Creator, Judge, and Redeemer), the divine governance, and our place in it. But he also held that God the Son, the Logos, or the divine will and wisdom, is active also beyond the flesh of the man Jesus before, during, and after the incarnation.[25] Thus, the Genevan Reformer did *not* claim that genuine knowledge of God and ourselves (the content of revelation) is available only to those who either know or encounter the man Jesus of Nazareth, and he did *not* claim that the true church is made up only of Christians. The implications of this for Reformed understandings of revelation and historical particularity are profound. Calvin had confessional theological reasons for claiming that the true knowledge of God and ourselves available to Christians in the particular historical person and event of Jesus of Nazareth was also available to others, e.g., the patriarchs, in other historically particular ways, e.g., the law.

H. Richard Niebuhr on revelation

H. Richard Niebuhr's mid-twentieth century American context was very different from Calvin's sixteenth century European one. Niebuhr cut his theological teeth during the 1930s not in the midst of Protestant reformation, but in a world gripped by economic depression, totalitarianism, and the Second World War. In *The Meaning of Revelation*, published in 1941, he tried to frame an understanding of revelation that could meet the challenges of *historical relativism* and *religious relativism*. By the former, he meant the recognition that our knowledge and experience are historically conditioned. By the latter, he meant the recognition that there is no neutrality in theology; whenever we speak and think significantly about something as god as well as about ourselves and other things in relation to it, we do so only from the point of view of faith in it. There are no neutral religious and theological statements because all religious and theological statements are relative to the object we take to be divine.

To meet these challenges, Niebuhr adopted what he called a "confessional method" in theology that proceeds from a particular viewpoint defined by the history of a specific community and its faith in a particular object of devotion.[26] So understood, a Christian theology views realities and objects from the historically particular perspective of the

Christian community, and it proceeds from that community's own account of its history with the God of Jesus Christ. Presumably, then, a confessional Muslim theology likewise would view things from the historically particular perspective of the Muslim community, and it would proceed from that community's own account of its history with the God of Mohammed, and so on.

Niebuhr also claimed that we are not blank paper when we encounter revelation in Jesus Christ. Instead, we come to this encounter with a worldview and an orientation in life already in place. That is, we bring with us an imaginative picture of things as well as a certain faith or devotion to one or another object or cause. Most often, the worldview that we bring, said Niebuhr, is one in which we imagine ourselves, our communities, and the things that we value at the center of things. By contrast, the revelation of God in Jesus Christ puts us, our communities, and the things that we value into the wider and displacing context of devotion to God and God's reign. (Indeed, Niebuhr noted, the image of the cross suggests "a total picture of significant action in which the self no longer occupies the center.")[27]

Or, to put this differently, according to Niebuhr, revelation in Jesus Christ triggers a conversion in our usual understanding of God and ourselves. Ordinarily, we live our lives in relation to many cherished objects, such as self, companions, family, nation, culture, beauty, and truth. In the push and shove of nature and history, all of these goods are threatened, and so the meaning of our lives is rendered insecure. We therefore long for a reality that will conserve ourselves and our values. We search for a *Jupiter Optimus Maximus* who will guarantee their continued existence, ensure them against mortality, and thus secure our lives and their meaning. Our usual ideas of divine unity, power, and goodness reflect this search and its implicit demand for a cosmic guarantor. Our ordinary or natural religion, then, is our great self-defense, our existential attempt to preserve ourselves, our life-orientations, and the many things that we value.

Ordinarily, then, we conceive the high god as a single principle that brings *unity* to the many things we value and that establishes an ordering of goods according to our own plan. But the God disclosed in Jesus Christ is not only the source of unities in our life. This God is also the enemy of the lesser unities of self, family, nation, and so on, whenever, in virtue of our self-serving pieties, we elevate them into false absolutes.[28] Again, Niebuhr maintained, the god we anticipate is like the powers of the world only raised to an ultimate degree, and our usual religious practice tries to enlist the help of this supreme power in order to overcome the world and its threats. But, in Jesus Christ, the power of God "is made perfect in weakness," and this disclosure "is the beginning of a revolution in our power thinking and our power politics."[29] Finally, said Niebuhr, we require that the deity be good in the sense that it protect and nourish the many other goods, e.g., self, family, nation, that we already cherish and adore. Revelation in Jesus Christ discloses a good God in relation to which we may center our lives and also estimate other things of value, but the goodness of this God is not a good that we love because it fulfills *our* quest for something to protect the other goods that we already love. Instead, we are met by a self-emptying goodness that convicts us "of having corrupted our religious life through our unquenchable desire to keep ourselves with our love of our good in the center of the picture."[30]

For Niebuhr, revelation in Jesus Christ represents the conversion of our natural religion, a redirection of our devotion toward divine reality that cannot be reduced to our stratagems of self-defense. It precipitates a reorientation of our lives toward the true God and it leads to a re-envisioning in relation to this God of ourselves and the many objects and others with which we interact. As he put it his essay on *Radical Monotheism and Western Culture*, what comes to expression in Jesus Christ is an uncompromising devotion to God that displaces self from the center of the picture, a devotion that also comes to expression in Judaism as well as in some Greek philosophy.[31] Thus, here we come across a theological pattern that has strong affinities with Calvin's reflections on the knowledge of God and of ourselves as well as his conviction that, as portrayed in both the Old Testament and the New, the purpose of human life is to glorify God.

H. Richard Niebuhr on the purpose of the church

Niebuhr published *The Purpose of the Church and Its Ministry: Reflections on the Aims of Theological Education* in 1956 as Part 1 of the Study of Theological Education in the United States and Canada sponsored by the American Association of Theological Schools. In it he did not offer a full or detailed doctrine of the church so much as an outline sufficient to frame a discussion of ministry and seminary education. Even so, his reflections in this book point to an expansive vision of the church and its purpose that clarifies his understanding of the historically particular revelation of God in Jesus Christ.

The church, said Niebuhr, is the subject that distinguishes itself from God, but that also apprehends the divine object and thus remains indispensable for human relations to that reality. As such, it is a community with a distinct spirit and way of life as well as an institution with many functions and offices. It is local and universal. It embraces both "the principle of protest against every tendency to confuse the symbol with what it symbolizes and the subject with the object," and "the principle of catholicity" or incarnation which affirms that the Infinite may be represented in finite, visible forms.[32] The world, the church's companion, "with which it lives before God," and to which it stands in a dynamic and complex relationship, is its foe, sometime partner, and frequent antagonist. But it is always "the community to which the Church addresses itself with its gospel, to which it gives an account of what it has seen and heard in divine revelation, [and] which it invites to come and see and hear."[33]

So understood, said Niebuhr, the church has many aims and objectives, from preaching and administering sacraments to developing caring communities and engaging in missions, and these multiply as soon as one considers the particular objectives of boards and departments, committees and classes, differently situated congregations and specialized ministries. But Niebuhr also believed that, beyond these many aims, there is an ultimate goal and objective, one "final unifying consideration that modifies all the special strivings," although he also noted that any statement of it must be personal and that we never achieve a final statement.[34] The chief end of the church, he said, may be expressed as the reconciliation of God and humanity, the acceptance of the gospel, or the realization of the kingdom. But there is no substitute for Jesus' own language; the ultimate purpose of the church is *"the increase among men of the love of God and neighbor."*[35]

Love of God and neighbor, said Niebuhr, is law and requirement, as expressed in the two tables of the Decalogue, Jesus' double summary of the law, and the shape of his life and ministry, but it is also gospel or the gift of grace that empowers and redirects us toward God and others. Love of God and neighbor—the two motifs are inseparable, said Niebuhr, since "the thought of God is impossible without the thought of the neighbor," and since the true meaning and worth of the neighbor depends on God.[36] In a lyrical passage, Niebuhr noted that love is rejoicing at the presence of the beloved, as well as gratitude, reverence and respect for the beloved, and loyalty to the beloved. He said that God is nothing less than "the Source and Center of all being...God the father Almighty, maker of Heaven and Earth." The human problem, then, is how to love this One "from whom death proceeds as well as life...who sets us in a world where our beloved neighbors are the objects of seeming animosity, who appears to us as God of wrath as well as God of love."[37] In fact, said Niebuhr, the problem of human life is how to be reconciled to God, and "reconciliation to God is reconciliation to life itself." Reconciliation means turning to God, a loyalty to God and to the things of God, "the patriotism of the universal commonwealth" displacing constricted loves to closed societies that render us disloyal to those beyond their borders and boundaries.[38] Reconciliation means being caught in the grips of an expansive love of God and neighbor, and so, in the light of reconciliation, my neighbor is near and far, friend and enemy, the one in need, the oppressed, the compassionate, the stranger, father, mother, sister, and brother. In the neighbor we see the redeemer "as in a glass darkly." My neighbor is past, present, and future. "He is man and he is angel and he is animal and inorganic being, all that participates in [God's universal community of] being."[39]

With this expansive passion in mind, Niebuhr then made a series of normative judgments directed against the negative effects on theological education of constricted understandings of the church and its purpose. Where a branch of the church, say a denomination, displaces the church in its wholeness as the environment for a seminary's work, theological education becomes provincial. Where the church (or Christianity), even considered as a whole, becomes the ultimate context for theological education, the church's work may be confused with the work of its Lord, and loyalty to God's kingdom may be equated with (and reduced to) loyalty to the church. Theological education then "becomes indoctrination in Christian principles rather than inquiry based on faith in God; or it is turned into training in methods for increasing the Church rather than for guiding men to love of God and neighbor."[40] Or again, the Bible, which remains indispensable for theological study, may be "so made the center of theological education that the book takes the place of devotion to the One who makes himself known with its aid." This, however, amounts to "a denial of the content of the Scriptures themselves," and so involves theological education in serious contradictions.[41] Finally, Christology may be substituted for theology, love of Jesus for love of God, and "life in the community of Jesus Christ for life in the divine commonwealth."[42] This, Niebuhr maintained, entails a misconstrual of Jesus' own witness as well as of Trinitarian conviction, and it introduces manifold internal conflicts into church and theological education. Indeed, it leads "to the effort to emphasize the uniqueness of the Christian religion, to define it as the 'true' religion, to recommend it because of its originality, to exaggerate the differences between Christian and Jewish faith, to re-erect walls of division that Jesus Christ broke down, to exalt followers of the one who humbled himself, to define the neighbor as fellow Christian."[43]

To summarize, for H. Richard Niebuhr, the historically particular revelation of God in Jesus Christ had a specific shape and pattern. Jesus is self-emptying; he points to God and God's reign. He is the one who holds fast in his loyalty to the almighty God who creates all things and to this God's universal commonwealth or kingdom even unto death on a cross. He is the one who teaches love of God and neighbor, and whose life and teaching extend love of neighbor even to enemies. In the frame of this particular revelation, then, Niebuhr claimed that the purpose of the church is best understood as the increase among persons of the love of God and neighbor, and he therefore also claimed that the church's mission cannot be reduced to increasing the church or to converting people to Christianity. The Christologically authorized and capacious point of the church is not to commend itself but God and the universal commonwealth of all persons and creatures and things in relation to God.

A broad pattern

Both John Calvin and H. Richard Niebuhr insist on the critical significance of the historically particular revelation of God in Jesus Christ, although neither claims that there is no true knowledge of God apart from Jesus of Nazareth. For Calvin, revelation in Jesus Christ brings a true knowledge of God's goodness and benevolence that, in our corrupted state, we fail to gain either from the seed of religion within us or the divine theatre round about us. This knowledge turns persons toward God and God's glory. For Niebuhr, revelation in Jesus Christ challenges the typical ideas of divine unity, power, and goodness that we concoct in our usual quest for a cosmic guarantor. It therefore represents the conversion of our natural religion as well as the redirection of human life toward the expansive reality of God and God's commonwealth.

In these ways, both Calvin and Niebuhr illustrate a broad and, for some of us, at least, also a compelling pattern of theological reflection that sometimes comes to expression in the Reformed sub-tradition of Christianity. The true knowledge of God and ourselves—the knowledge of God's disposition toward us and toward all things and the knowledge of our place in the divine commonwealth as participants and beneficiaries of grace—reorients human life toward a reality considerably greater than ourselves and our closed communities. And, we hope, it is this reorientation that will dispose the church of Jesus Christ to take up ever more faithful and generous postures toward the many other creatures, persons, and historic communities in God's world.

Notes

1. Brunner, Emil, *The Divine Imperative*, Translated by Olive Wyon (Philadelphia: Westminster Press, 1937), pp. 51–60, 291ff. *Natural Theology*, Edited by John Baillie (London: Geoffrey Bles, 1946), pp. 71–2; Karl Barth, *Church Dogmatics*, Translated by G. W. Bromiley (Edinburgh: T. & T. Clark, 1975), 1/1: 6, 72.
2. Not to mention movements and institutions the "Christianness" of which is often contested, such as Unitarians and Mormons.
3. Calvin, John, *Institutes of the Christian Religion*, Translated by Ford Lewis Battles, Edited by John T. McNeill (Louisville: Westminster John Knox Press, 1960), p. 35.
4. Ibid., pp. 40, 41.
5. Ibid., p. 6.
6. Calvin, *Institutes*, p. 1,521. The first question of Calvin's own Geneva Catechism reads as follows. "*Minister*. 'What is the chief end of human life?' *Child*. 'To know God.'" See *Our Confessional Heritage: Confessions of the Reformed Tradition With a Contemporary Declaration of Faith* (Atlanta: The Presbyterian Church in the United States, 1978), p. 19. Question #1 of the Shorter Catechism asks "What is the chief end of man?" The catechumen is to answer, "To glorify God and enjoy him forever." *The Book of Confessions: Study Edition* (Geneva Press, 1999), p. 229.
7. Calvin, *Institutes*, 51, 53.

8. "Wherever you cast your eyes, there is no spot in the universe wherein you cannot discern at least some sparks of his glory." Calvin, *Institutes*, p. 52. See also p. 58.
9. Calvin, *Institutes*, pp. 48–9, 55–6.
10. Calvin, *Institutes*, p. 1,153.
11. Calvin, *Institutes*, pp. 1,155–6.
12. Calvin, *Institutes*, pp. 69–70.
13. Calvin, *Institutes*, pp. 1,016–21.
14. Calvin, *Institutes*, pp. 1,173–7.
15. *Book of Confessions*, pp. 93–96.
16. *Book of Confessions*, p. 43.
17. Calvin, *Institutes*, pp. 343, 431, 434–7.
18. Calvin, *Institutes*, p. 1,337.
19. Calvin, *Institutes*, p. 429.
20. Calvin, *Institutes*, pp. 434–5.
21. Calvin, *Institutes*, p. 348.
22. Calvin, *Institutes*, p. 427.
23. Calvin, *Institutes*, p. 462.
24. *Book of Confessions*, pp. 34–5.
25. This is the so-called *extra calvinisticum*. See Oberman, Heiko Augustus, *The Dawn of the Reformation: Essays in Later Medieval and Early Reformation Thought* (Edinburgh: T&T Clark, 1986), pp. 239, 247. E. David Willis notes that the term was probably introduced during the 1620s. See *Calvin's Catholic Christology: The Function of the So-Called Extra Calvinisticum in Calvin's Theology* (Leiden: E. J. Brill, 1966), pp. 9, 23.
26. Niebuhr, H. Richard, *The Meaning of Revelation* (Louisville: Westminster John Knox, 2006), p. 21.
27. Ibid., p. 65.
28. Ibid., p. 96.
29. Ibid., p. 98.
30. Ibid., p. 99.
31. Niebuhr, H. Richard, *Radical Monotheism and Western Culture With Supplementary Essays* (Louisville: Westminster John Knox, 1993), pp. 39–42.
32. Niebuhr, H. Richard, *The Purpose of the Church and Its Ministry: Reflections on the Aims of Theological Education* (New York: Harper & Brothers, 1956), p. 25.
33. Ibid., p. 26.
34. Ibid., pp. 29, 32.
35. Ibid., p. 31.
36. Niebuhr, Ibid., p. 33. The rich dynamic of love of God and neighbor was one that, for Niebuhr, lay near the heart of Christology. Thus, in *Christ and Culture* (New York: Harper, 1951), pp. 28–9, Niebuhr noted that the sonship of Jesus Christ "involves the double movement—with men toward God, with God toward men; from the world to the Other, from the Other to the world; from work to Grace, from Grace to work; from time to the Eternal and from the Eternal to the temporal."
37. Niebuhr, *The Purpose of the Chruch and Its Ministry*, p. 36.
38. Ibid., p. 37.

39. Ibid., p. 38.
40. Ibid., p. 43.
41. Ibid., p. 43.
42. Ibid., p. 44.
43. Ibid., p. 46.

JEWS AND GENTILES IN THE DIVINE ECONOMY

P. Mark Achtemeier

In the aftermath of the *Scandal of Particularity* dialogue, I am convinced that Jewish-Christian relations can be fostered and enhanced by those of us on the Christian side learning to grasp more firmly and in the right way some of the core insights of our Christianity. Christianity and Judaism both embrace historical particularity in their religious claims, and such particularity can indeed be a source of scandal. But it can also provide an impetus for closer and more peaceful relations, as I hope to show with these reflections.

As my starting point I want to lift up a statement from St. Athanasius of Alexandria, a fourth-century theologian who was engaged in a foundational debate about how one ought to refer to God in the liturgy:

> Therefore it will be much more accurate to denote God from the Son and to call Him Father, than to name Him and call Him Unoriginated from His works only.[1]

Athanasius here argues against theological opponents who are seeking to ground liturgical practice in abstract philosophical understandings of God as the uncreated origin of all things. Athanasius argues to the contrary, that the most accurate and reliable understandings of God are those which are grounded in the *particular history of God's interactions with the world*, most notably in the incarnation.

Athanasius' statement is emblematic of the path Christian theology followed in the defining debates surrounding the fourth-century councils of Nicaea and Constantinople, which together laid the foundations for the doctrines of the Incarnation and the Trinity. In a nutshell, the Christian tradition learned to subject all inherited understandings of God to a thoroughgoing re-evaluation and revision in light of what the church understood to be God's actual appearing in history in Jesus of Nazareth and the Holy Spirit. Through the work of Athanasius and his allies, the grounding source for Christian understandings of God became not philosophy, but the divine *economy*,[2] a technical term signifying the concrete, historical particulars of God's interaction with the world.

This determination to ground religious knowledge in the history of God's particular interactions with human beings is obviously a trait that Christianity shares with much of Judaism. The existence of the Jewish people is the result of God's particular election of Abraham and his offspring. As the premise of our dialogue recognized clearly, this reliance on historical particulars of the divine economy is inherently scandalous. Claims that God elects this people and not that one, appears to one group of disciples and not another, are troublesome for persons and groups who stand outside the focal points of the economy or who read the history differently.

Different understandings of Jesus' place in the divine economy obviously give rise to key disagreements between Jews and Christians, but I want to claim that a determined focus on the divine economy can also serve as a key resource for fostering sympathetic and respectful relations between Christians and Jews. In order to develop this claim, I will be drawing on work presented to the *Scandal of Particularity* group by Kendall Soulen. But first some preliminaries:

As will become clear in due course, my starting point in developing these reflections is explicitly Christian, and not of a sort that Jews would likely agree with. My goal here is not to develop a least-common-denominator understanding that Jews and Christians could all sign on to, doubtless at considerable cost to their respective religious identities. My aim is rather to offer explicitly Christian reflections that help to provide theological warrant for a respectful, mutually appreciative engagement with Jews.

In developing its own distinctive understandings of God and God's way with the world, historic Christianity has attended very closely to the "economic" particulars of Jesus' life, death and resurrection, and the community's encounters with the Holy Spirit. Quite striking, however, is how little theological attention has been paid to the historical reality of the Jews as a people enduring through time. What impact would it have on Christian understandings of God, and what possibilities would it open up for Christian-Jewish relations, if the "economic" character of Christianity asserted itself in this arena as well? What would be the implications of also taking seriously the historical persistence of the Jewish people and Jewish identity through time as part of the divine economy?

The obstacle to this kind of theologically serious engagement with the enduring history of the Jews has historically been the supercessionist theologies which developed early on in the church's history. The General Assembly of my own Presbyterian Church (U.S.A.) describes such theologies in a critique from a 1987 statement:

> Supercessionism maintains that because the Jews refused to receive Jesus the Messiah, they were cursed by God, are no longer in covenant with God, and that the church alone is the "true Israel" or the "spiritual Israel."[3]

These "theologies of replacement" interpret God's promises of land and offspring to Abraham as having been spiritually fulfilled in the church. From a supercessionist perspective, Abraham's carnal descendents, the Jews, thus have no further theological significance in the historically unfolding plan of God, save perhaps as an object of missionary efforts.

If supercessionist theology were correct, it would seem reasonable to expect that the Jewish people, having fulfilled their God-given role as bearers of the "Old Covenant" and supplanted finally by the church, would be scattered and absorbed among the nations, eventually to disappear from the stage of history as an identifiable group. That this has *not* been the way Jewish history has unfolded, despite many centuries of determined persecution, is theologically striking.

Christians have recognized the striking character of this development, and have made limited use of it in their own efforts to defend and promote belief in God. Walker Percy provides an apt illustration of this when asks in one of his essays, "*Where are the Hittites?*"

> Why does no one find it remarkable that in most world cities today there are Jews but not one single Hittite even though the Hittites had a great flourishing civilization while the Jews nearby were a weak and obscure people?
>
> When one meets a Jew in New York or New Orleans or Paris or Melbourne, it is remarkable that no one considers the event remarkable. What are they doing here? But it is even more remarkable to wonder, if there are Jews here, why are there not Hittites here?[4]

Percy makes this point in the service of a general argument for the existence of a God who is actively engaged in human history. That the argument works well in that context, however, underscores its potential significance for broader Christian understandings of the place of the Jews in the divine economy. If history has so dramatically failed to unfold as supercessionist theologies would have led one to expect, should that fact in itself not serve to raise serious questions about the validity of supercessionist assumptions?

A word about the hazards of this type of theological reasoning is in order before proceeding further. The easy identification of God's will and intention with the unfolding course of human history is an exercise fraught with moral and intellectual hazard. Karl Barth quite rightly pronounced his famous "*Nein*" ("No!") against attempts to derive knowledge of God from empirical observations of creatures—nature and history. Barth was acutely aware of these dangers, writing as he was in a context where Hitler's rise to power had been interpreted by too many German Christians as *prima-facie* evidence of God's intention to bless and fulfill the destiny of the Aryan race.[5]

But a cautious reluctance to derive theological conclusions from historical observations cannot become absolute. The rise of particular rulers or empires is surely a different matter than the historical persistence through millennia of a people claiming to be blessed and chosen by God. In addition, there is explicit precedent within the Christian canon for drawing conclusions about the divine economy from the unfolding history of the Jews: Paul's discussion in Romans 11 interprets even so problematic a development as Israel's rejection of faith in Jesus as a positive expression of the will and plan of God, one that opens the door for the conversion of the Gentiles and moves toward final redemption for Jew and Gentile alike.

What, then, might the effect be on Christian understandings of God if the ongoing, historical existence of "carnal Israel" were understood as part of the divine economy, a positive component of God's ultimate plan for dealing with the human race and human history as a whole? Kendall Soulen, in *The God of Israel and Christian Theology*, has provided a groundbreaking proposal about what such a theology might look like.[6] The scope of this essay will not do it justice, but at the heart of Soulen's proposal is a shift in the emphasis of Christian theology away from its historical emphasis on God's work as Redeemer, delivering humanity from sin and guilt on the cross, in favor of God's work as a Consummator, who works for the renewing and perfecting of creation in accordance with a plan that was in place from the very beginning.

Soulen is determined then to read the history of God's election of Israel not, as Christianity has classically done, as part of the history of redemption, but as an integral part of God's consummating intention for the world. Put differently, Soulen sees the election of Abraham and his offspring not primarily as God's response to humanity's fall into sin, but as the concrete historical expression of an original divine intention to differentiate the human race into the categories of Jew and Gentile, Israel and the nations.

Hewing closely to the divine promises given to Abraham in Genesis 12, Soulen emphasizes that this differentiation of humanity does not mean that God's blessing is limited, but it does mean that God intends divine blessing to come in a different way to the Gentiles than it does to Israel, precisely through Israel's calling to be a light to the nations.

> To be a Gentile is to be the other of Israel and as such an indispensable partner in a single economy of blessing that embraces the whole human family. This does not mean that Israel alone will bless the nations or the nations alone will bless Israel. God is the ultimate source of blessing for both. But God blesses both as the God of Israel, and hence in the context of the history that unfolds on the basis of the distinction between Israel and "all the families of the earth."[7]

If this is in fact the way God chooses to deal with humanity from the very beginning, then a supercessionist view which saw the church as replacing Israel in God's plan would in fact constitute a denial of God's fundamental purpose for the redemption of the world.

But why, Soulen asks, would God choose to deal with the human race as twofold? What is there about this kind of differentiated existence that serves the divine will for the consummation and perfection of creation?

> In reply, one might observe that a blessing is by its very nature something imparted from one to an *other*. As such, blessing presupposes difference. When difference disappears, so too does the possibility of genuine blessing.[8]

Soulen argues that this pattern of mutual blessing within a context of difference is essential to the kind of world consummated in love that God intends from the very beginning of creation.

It is important to emphasize that Soulen's proposal does *not* do away with the significance of Christ's sacrifice on the cross as the center of God's work for the redemption of creation from the powers of sin and evil. But Soulen does seek to locate the work of redemption within the larger context of God's consummating will, seeing redemption as a response necessitated by humanity's fall into sin. The purpose of God's redemption of the world is to remove the barriers which sin and evil place in the way of God's original consummating will, and thus to make possible the fulfillment of creation in loving, differentiated blessing in accordance with God's original intention.

Soulen's proposal is impressive as a constructive attempt at a non-supercessionist reading of Christianity, one that takes seriously the ongoing existence of the Jewish people as an essential part of the divine economy. For all its strengths, however, one might question whether Soulen provides an adequate answer to the question why it is so important to God to bifurcate the human race into two as a pre-requisite of the consummation of creation. Soulen's answer, cited above, is that mutual blessing requires difference, but with so many obvious differences present already among members of the human race, it is not obvious why this additional one, between Jew and Gentile, should serve as a *sine qua non* for creation to achieve its divinely desired consummation. At the end of the day one wonders if this point about the connection between blessing and difference is not asked to carry more systematic weight than it is rightly able to bear. As a result Soulen's proposal runs the danger of taking on a kind of ad hoc flavor, seeming more the product of a (commendable) desire for a Christianity to develop an alternative to its supercessionist heritage than a proposal that is systematically compelling in its own right.

Soulen's argument might be placed on more secure foundations by connecting it more broadly with the understanding of the divine economy that stands at the heart of Christian faith. I refer of course to the economic manifestations of the incarnate Christ and the Holy Spirit which in Christian view disclose fullness of divine reality. The result is the doctrine of the Trinity, which treats the historical communion of Jesus and the Father in the Spirit as a genuine disclosure in time and history of the mystery of the eternal divine nature. The one God of Israel is revealed in the fullness of time as the eternal, loving communion of these three, Father, Son and Spirit.

One of the striking features of Soulen's description of God's will for the consummation of creation in terms of mutual blessing within a structure of difference, is the extent to which his language echoes that of Trinitarian theology: In the confession of the one God as Father, Son and Holy Spirit, the church proclaims difference-as-blessing to be the primordial ground of all reality. John Milbank describes well the "ontology of peace" that stands at the heart of the church's Trinitarian faith:

> Christianity...recognizes no original violence. It construes the infinite not as chaos, but as harmonic peace which is yet beyond the circumscribing power of any totalizing reason. Peace no longer depends on the reduction to the self-identical, but is the *sociality* of harmonious difference... Christianity...is the coding of transcendental difference as peace.[9]

The similarity in language is highly suggestive. Is it possible to forge a link between understandings of God grounded in the Trinitarian economy, and Soulen's proposal for the shape of God's consummating will in the relations of mutual blessing and difference constituted by the differentiation of the human race into Jew and Gentile?

One possibility for how to do this may be suggested by an early fifth-century work of St. Augustine on the doctrine of the Trinity.[10] Augustine in that work sought to link the understanding of God as triune with the scriptural affirmation that human beings are created in the image of God. The result was a highly influential quest for images of the Trinity residing within the structure of individual human consciousness. Augustine found a number of suggestive triads, eventually deciding that the most satisfactory of these images, though still inadequate in significant respects, was the mutually interdependent relationships of memory, will and understanding within the unified consciousness of a single human being.

In the spirit of Augustine, we might pose the question whether the image of the triune God could fruitfully be sought, not just within individual human beings, but within collective human existence as well. Could Soulen's suggestion, that mutual blessing within a human existence differentiated as Jew and Gentile, be seen as an image of the loving differentiation-within-unity that characterizes the Trinitarian understanding of God?

But a proper image of the Trinity of course requires three. Where is the third member of this differentiated communion to be found? Surely that third One from whose blessing both Jew and Gentile receive their fundamental identity is none other than God himself.

It might of course be objected that viewing God as one of the three is illegitimate if the goal is to find the image of the Triune God within collective *human* existence. But in light of the Christian affirmation that God has appeared incarnate among us as a particular human being, this objection would appear not to hold. In fact, such an affirmation would give added resonance to historic Christian affirmations that Jesus of Nazareth in his own person represents the perfection of the divine image within human nature.

If the Trinitarian divine image is in fact discernible in the reality and promise of Jew and Gentile standing in differentiated relations of mutual blessing with God and with one another, then the logic for viewing the historical persistence of the Jewish people as an integral part of the divine economy becomes practically irresistible. God's consummating work can now be understood not simply in terms of an abstract concept of mutual blessing, but as the perfection of the divine image within the universal human community. In line with Soulen's proposal, this perfection of the divine image has as its necessary pre-condition the differentiation of the one human race into Jew and Gentile. And the quest for peaceful relations of mutual blessing between Jews and Gentiles can now be seen as much more than simply a practical necessity or an ethical ideal: it is in the strongest possible sense, the perfection of the human creature according to God's original creative will, an indispensable component of God's plan for the fulfillment and consummation of creation.

If this line of thinking is correct, it will have major implications for how Christians think about issues of proselytism and conversion as regards the Jewish people. Bringing Jews to the Gospel cannot be faithfully consonant with God's will if it means the absorption of the Jewish people into the church with a consequent loss of Jewish identity. Helpful in this connection is Soulen's approving citation of Michael Wyschogrod's reflections on the subject:

> For Wyschogrod, the acid test of the church's theological posture toward Israel's election is the church's conduct toward Jews who have been baptized. For it is here that the church demonstrates in an ultimate way whether it understands itself in light of God's eternal covenant with the seed of Abraham. If the church acknowledges the abiding reality of Israel's corporeal election, it will naturally expect baptized Jews to maintain faithfully their Jewish identity.[11]

The church cannot renounce the proclamation of the Gospel and maintain its identity as the church. But if the consummation of God's will for human beings requires the presence of Jews and Gentiles praising God together, then the Gospel proclaimed cannot take the form of a command or even an invitation to renounce Jewish identity.

I am acutely aware coming to the end of these reflections that the ideas I have put forward will be inaccessible to my Jewish colleagues, dependent as I have been upon Christian understandings of the divine economy culminating in the doctrine of the Trinity.

But it is also worth considering, I believe, whether we might discern images of that differentiated unity harmonized as peace which we have been discussing as we observe members of separate religious traditions working in parallel with one another, each seeking to develop theologically coherent accounts of the other using language and thought-forms consistent with their own tradition, and each seeking to shape those accounts in a way that links faithfulness to the one God with the development of harmonious and mutually benevolent relations toward the other. Though my Jewish friends may not resonate with my use of Trinitarian doctrine, it is my hope, confirmed in encounter through the *Scandal of Particularity* dialogue, that they will develop resources out of their own tradition for understanding Gentile existence in the plan of God, with the goal of our arriving together at a place of mutual blessing and praise offered to the God of Abraham.

Notes

1. Saint Athanasius, "Defence of the Nicene Definition (De Decretis)," ch.vii, sec. 31, in *A Select Library of Nicene and Post-Nicene Father of the Church: Second Series*, reprint edition, vol. 4, ed. Philip Schaaf (Grand Rapids: Eerdmans, 1952-54), 171, cited in *Speaking the Christian God*, ed. Alvin F. Kimel Jr. (Grand Rapids, MI: Eerdmans, 1992), 132.
2. From the Greek *oikonomia*, the administration of a household's affairs.
3. *Christians and Jews: People of God*, Church Issues Series, No. 7 (Louisville: Presbyterian Church (U.S.A.) Office of Theology and Worship), 12.
4. Percy, Walker, *The Message in the Bottle*, 1st Picador edition (New York: Picador U.S.A., 2000), 6.
5. *Natural Theology: Comprising "Nature and Grace" By Professor Dr. Emil Brunner and the Reply "No!" By Dr. Karl Barth*, trans. Peter Fraenkl (London: The Centenary Press, 1946).
6. Soulen, R. Kendall, *The God of Israel and Christian Theology* (Minneapolis: Fortress Press, 1996).
7. Ibid., 125-6.
8. Ibid., 134.
9. Milbank, John, *Theology and Social Theory* (Malden, MA: Blackwell Publishers, 1990), 5-6.
10. Saint Augustine, *The Trinity (De Trinitate)*, trans. Edmund Hill, O.P. (Hyde Park, NY: New City Press, 1991).
11. Soulen, 11.

"HE UNROLLED THE SCROLL...AND HE ROLLED UP THE SCROLL AND GAVE IT BACK"

Samuel E. Balentine

Perhaps the most commonplace contemporary portrait of Judaism is the picture of devout Jews standing at the Western Wall of the remains of the Temple in Jerusalem reading a Torah scroll. The central components of this familiar image are a building and a book. Their association with one another is so conventional that the ironies and contradictions of their filiation can easily go unnoticed. Although they share common values and concerns, the building and the book exhibit divergent traits. The building is fixed; the book is portable. The book is read outside the building; its recitation parallels the rites practiced within. The book describes the rituals inside the building but is not part of them. The building requires lineage; the book demands literacy...the complex relationships between the building and the book—the Temple and the Torah—constitute the foundation of Judaism.[1]

This quote introduces William Scott Green's article on "Levitical Religion." His objective is to show that the destruction of the Temple in Jerusalem in 586 BCE "was not the end of Israel's Temple-centered religion of cult and sacrifice." It was not the end, because during the exile Israel's priestly leadership gathered and edited the community's national traditions—narratives about its origins and destiny along with a set of behavioral principles and practices that defined its life in relationship to God and the world—into a text, which Judaism now recognizes as the Torah. The Torah was not a replacement for a lost religion; it was a compensation, an interim strategy for obedience to God in a world where politics and power had destroyed the very symbols that had once secured and nourished life in God's presence. Green observes that although the Torah *preserved* a collective memory, it also *modified*, and more importantly *transformed* it. Now, the promulgation of a text, not a temple or an altar, serves as a guide to religious practice. In short, "Reading the Torah becomes a means for the Jews to relate to God."[2]

A second citation from Green sharpens the point:

> Through the Torah, the Israelites in exile could relate to the Temple's religion of cult and sacrifice by reading about it, by hearing about it, by thinking about it, but not by actually performing it. Mary Douglas envisions this as follows: "There is no tabernacle, the faithful are not moving around in it, all the movement is in the book they are reading, or hearing through their ears. Learning the book becomes a way of internalizing the tabernacle..." The Torah evoked a religion that Israel could not directly experience. In the religion it constitutes, the Torah becomes in itself what is described in the text, a portable point of contact between God and Israel, a textual Tabernacle.[3]

Green's image of the complex relationship between "the building and the book" in Judaism set me to thinking. What would be the analog for Christianity? Several possibilities come to mind. We might think, for example, of one of the Protestant reformers (in this context, John Calvin, of course) reading Holy Writ from a grand church pulpit in Europe; of the Pope reading scripture at Saint Peter's; or—and I apologize for this abrupt segue—of a Billy Graham crusade in Candlestick Park, of William Sloan Coffin preaching at Riverside Church in New York, of Robert Schuller preaching in the Crystal Cathedral, even Jerry Falwell, holding forth in Lynchburg, VA, with surround sound and video streaming, of course, to people and places far beyond. These and other images surely contribute to a portrait of the complex relationship between the Bible and the Church in contemporary Christianity. I have chosen to look elsewhere, however.

The Gospel of Luke offers the following description of Jesus reading scripture in Nazareth. Whether or not it has contemporary significance is, I suggest, a question that lies at the heart of the issue we have met to consider.

> When he came to Nazareth, where he had been brought up, he went to the synagogue on the sabbath day, as was his custom. He stood up to read, and the scroll of the prophet Isaiah was given to him. He unrolled the scroll and found the place where it was written:
>
> "The Spirit of the Lord is upon me,
>   because he has anointed me to bring good news to the poor.
> He has sent me to proclaim release to the captives
>   and recovery of sight to the blind,
>   to let the oppressed go free,
> to proclaim the year of the Lord's favor."
>
> And he rolled up the scroll, gave it back to the attendant, and sat down. The eyes of all in the synagogue were fixed on him. Then he began to say to them, "Today this scripture has been fulfilled in your hearing." All spoke well of him and were amazed at the gracious words that came from his mouth. (Luke 4:16–22)

Discerning a model for reading and hearing scripture

Luke's text invites consideration of several issues, each of which may contribute to (and problematize) a model for thinking about the authority of scripture in the modern world.

Context and setting

Luke reports that following his baptism by John, Jesus began his ministry in Nazareth. Luke does not make much of this location, and on first read we may be tempted to treat it as an incidental detail. It is instructive to remember, however, that Nazareth is a specific place on the map, and it provides a concrete setting for the reading and hearing of scripture. It is a Jewish village in the Lower Galilee, nestled inconspicuously between the Jezreel valley to the south, the Mediterranean Sea to the west, and the Sea of Galilee to the east. It is the village of Mary and Joseph, the place where Jesus "had been brought up" (4:16), the place where a small community of friends and neighbors (likely no more than 500) knew him as "Joseph's boy" (4:22). The date of Jesus' return to his hometown is unspecified, but we know that the calendar is turned to the first decades of the first century, a time period when daily life throughout Palestine was defined by Roman rule. In the metropolitan areas of the Empire, for example in cities like Rome, Alexandria, and Jerusalem, we know that the Romans permitted the Jews a measure of autonomy. As long as they were not subversive, they were free to participate in the marketplace of ideas and opportunities provided by a blended Greco-Roman culture. In smaller villages like Nazareth, we may assume that such opportunities were more abstract than actual. Local synagogues sustained traditional practices in a world that tolerated religious conviction but did little to reward it. And even in the synagogues, according to the archeological evidence from the Galilee area, the visible symbols of Judaism had likely been amalgamated with images from a status-quo culture that diminished their claims on a people formed by distinctive memories. In sum, when Jesus unrolled, then read, the scroll of Isaiah in Nazareth, he addressed persons whose lives were shaped by both the present world and the past, but abiding, Word.

In the recommended readings you received for this conference, you have a pre-publication collection of essays on the authority of scripture edited by William P. Brown. In his "Introduction" to this collection, Brown observes that when it comes to scripture, "authority is domain specific." I take this to mean that whatever authority the Bible may have in the modern world, it must be persuasive in the real world of competing and viable alternatives. Neither in Nazareth nor in Richmond does the reading of scripture command automatic assent. Every word that claims to mediate a transcendent truth from God must compete for a hearing with other and different truths spoken by this-world authorities, who command and exert power that may be resisted but cannot be denied.

Once we concede that the Bible's authority is domain specific, another issue comes into view. Does a biblical text read by a first century Jewish community in Nazareth mean the same thing when it is read or heard by other communities in different times and places? Would merchants and artisans in Corinth, familiar with patrons devoted to the Egyptian goddess Isis parading through the city, have sufficient interest or reason to turn aside and listen to a word from a Jewish God? The response to Paul's preaching by the Epicurean and Stoic philosophers in Athens accents the question. "What does this babbler want to say?" He seems to be a proclaimer of foreign deities" (Acts 17:18). Once we move beyond the context and settings of the early church to the modern world, the problem becomes still more acute. What authority does the Bible have for tribal villagers in southern Sudan, for the Muslim in Indonesia, for the Buddhist in Sri Lanka, for the Hindu in Bombay? Or to bring the question closer to home, what transcendent truths about the world and humankind can the Bible offer to the modern secularist, who regards religious perspectives as irrelevant at best, dangerous and destructive, at worst?[4] If the Bible's authority is domain specific, and if there is a plurality of domains in which the modern world searches for truth, not only in time and place but also, for example, in religion and science, medicine and law, ethics and philosophy, then how can we be certain that what we hold as authoritative in one domain is equally authoritative in another?

Christianity has exemplified various ways to answer such questions. Traditional Catholicism cedes absolute authority to the institution of the Church. Classical Protestantism has resisted this model, insisting instead on the absolute authority of Scripture, the Word of God, mediated through the Holy Spirit and preserved by the *regula fidei* (rule of faith), which controls dissent by promoting allegiance to formulated confessions and creeds. Within Protestantism, primarily, Fundamentalism finds ultimate authority in the very words of scripture, whose inerrant truth provides insulation against every challenge modernity poses. We may debate the strengths and weaknesses of each of these approaches; indeed, almost any book you read on the authority of scripture will devote considerable attention to them. But it may be sufficient for our purposes simply to recognize that no one approach to how and why the Bible is authoritative across and within various contexts and settings has as yet proved persuasive.[5] Authoritative statements on the Bible's authority are seldom able to attain the authority they claim. The statement is redundant, of course, which makes its truth all the more unsettling.

Tradition

Luke reports that when Jesus came to Nazareth, "he went to the synagogue on the sabbath day, as was his custom" (4:16). By doing so, Jesus exemplifies a willing conformity to traditional habits of piety. The synagogue represents both an institutional *linkage* to the Temple and a *modification* of its function in society. The Temple is regarded as a holy place that assures effective access to the presence of God. The English word "synagogue" (from the LXX) most frequently translates Hebrew words meaning "congregation" or "assembly," which indicates that it functions more as a gathering place for people than as a (symbolic) residence for God.[6] There is no uniform picture of what occurred in the worship of the synagogue at the time of Jesus, but it likely included reading from the Torah and the prophets, exposition, and prayer. The synagogue clearly provides a central place that links Jews to important persons (Moses, according to Acts 15:21 and often in Rabbinic tradition; Ezra and Nehemiah, according to some theories of origin) and events in Israelite history (the exile, the restoration of Jerusalem). It also clearly reflects the change necessitated by the destruction of the Temple (in 586 and again in 70 CE)[7] and the cessation of the "Temple-centered religion of cult and sacrifice," to use Green's terms once again. The shift in emphasis indicates that within the synagogue, the encounter with God takes places in the midst of people assembled around the Word read, preached, taught, and prayed.

Jesus' decision to go to the synagogue on "the sabbath day" also signals his recognition of tradition's importance for nurturing and shaping religious behavior. Jewish observance of the sabbath is rooted in ancient Israel's creation theology (Gen.2:1–3), which envisions a holy day of rest and celebration as part of God's primordial plan for the cosmos. Its observance is formalized as a commandment in the pivotal revelation from God at Mt. Sinai (Exod.20:8–11; Deut.5:12–15), where it provides the linchpin that holds together Israel's covenantal commitment to love God absolutely (commandments 1–3) and to live among others in the world in full accordance with this love (commandments 5–10). The sabbath's imperative for worship of God that is inextricably coupled to enactments of justice in everyday life is the consistent burden of Israel's prophets (e.g., Amos 8:3–6; Isa.1:10–17; 56:2, 4, 6) and priests (see especially the requirements in Leviticus 25–26 concerning the Jubilee year, on which see below), and a promise of God's inviolable blessing, both to Israel and non-Israelites (e.g., Isa.56:1–8; 58:13–14; 66:22–23). The trajectory of the sabbath's importance is extended by Qumran texts (e.g., 4QShirShabb; CD VI, X-XII; 11QTemple), apocryphal and pseudepigraphical texts (e.g., Jub.2:17–33; 50:6–13; I Macc.2:29–31; II Macc.5:25–41), and extensively in rabbinic literature.

Luke's account of Jesus reading scripture on the sabbath day is but one example of the way the New Testament embraces its Jewish roots (cf. Matt.4:23; 9:35; Mark 1:21, 39; 6:2; Luke 6:6; John 6:59; 18:20; Acts 6:9). Luke's description of Jesus' conformity with tradition does not, however, provide a complete picture, for elsewhere the New Testament accents Jesus' debate with Jewish authorities concerning what work could or could not be done on this traditional day of rest. It is instructive to note that of the six texts that describe this debate, five deal with the question of healing on the Sabbath (Mark 3:1–6 and parallels; Luke 13:10–17; 14:1–6; John 5:1–9; 9:1–41) and one deals with the issue of plucking grain on the sabbath (Mark 2:23–26 and parallels). In each case, as a general rule, Jesus teaches that sabbath observance does not exempt one from the responsibility to heal those infirmed and to sustain those whose life is threatened. Yet, even as he critiques the tradition in which he participates, Jesus remains fully connected to it. When he asserts that "the Sabbath was made for humankind and not humankind for the sabbath (Mark 2:27), he both draws upon an Old Testament precedent (cf. Lev.24:5–9 and I Sam.21:2–6) and anticipates the teachings of the rabbis (e.g., *Tanhuma* 245a; *m. Shabbat* 16:1–7; 18:3; see also *Midrash on Exod* 31:12; *Exod Rabbah* 25:11; *Deut Rabbah* 1:21). In sum, when Luke reports that Jesus "went to the *synagogue* on the *sabbath* day," he not only locates Jesus within traditional beliefs and practices, he also invites us to understand that obedience to God often requires more than conformity to tradition.

Luke's account of Jesus' Galilean ministry provides insight into first century tensions between time-honored religious traditions and time-sensitive religious practices. Even so, whatever values we may cede to first century convictions about regularly setting aside days for reading and hearing words from scripture, there is strong evidence that such convictions, even among those who claim to be religious, are accorded little or no authority in the modern world. Two anecdotal observations suffice as illustration.

The most obvious Christian analog for the synagogue is the church, where Christians gather as a community to hear and heed the truths promulgated by scripture. Modernity has, however, seriously eroded almost all traditional notions of community, corporate commitment, and collective identity. Robert Putnam uses the leisure activity of bowling as a cipher for the assessment of our prevailing sense of disconnectedness. Once we bowled in leagues, striving for wins and bearing the losses with a team of kindred spirits. Now we not only bowl alone, we essentially live alone. We seldom make long-term commitments to anything beyond ourselves. We do not join bridge clubs, charity leagues, YWCA, PTA, political parties, or religious denominations. We may send a check, agree to make a call, have our name listed in a membership roll, but for the most part our participation in institutional organizations is more an addition to our resume than a substantive and active contribution to our lives. Our principal connection to anything outside our private domains is the internet, which enables us to download, use, and then delete prepackaged data that satisfies our personal needs and curiosities. The church, ever alert to new marketing devices, has of course tapped into this way of connecting with its patrons. We have eagerly moved from the traditional models of tele-evangelism to sophisticated video streaming of our worship services, jazzed-up web-pages with electronic links to ministry opportunities, and email server lists that help us stay connected, through widescreen monitors, to those we no longer sit beside on the pew. Today, we are just as likely to get our notions about what the Bible says from Google, Wikipedia, or the Discovery Channel, which one of my colleagues recently described as the "National Enquirer" of cable TV (e.g., its March 4, 2007 exposé on "The Lost Tomb of Jesus"). One wonders how the word "authority" has any measurable meaning at all in this setting.

The notion of sacred time, whether on the sabbath or any other day or season of the year, will also seem like a strange idea to many in the modern world. The notion that observance of sacred time contributes to cosmic harmony and social justice will seem to many like culturally sanctioned voodoo, New Age nonsense, or just plain silly, perhaps especially to those actively committed to social justice movements. When was the last time you saw a protestor carrying a placard that reads, "Work for Justice—Go to Worship"? (One often sees signs citing John

3:16, but does this not exacerbate our dis-ease with such a way of appealing to the Bible?) It may well have been the "custom" for Jesus and others in the first century to mark their week by going to the synagogue on the sabbath, but there is little evidence that this norm transfers automatically to us. In the ongoing press to be good "time-managers," we learn, almost in self-defense, to *schedule our work* in the hope that there may some *time left over for our rest*. When we open our calendars to mark the appointments around which we schedule our lives, we instinctively look for Monday to Friday, typically 9 am–5 pm, although both boundaries for the work week are constantly eroding. To be sure, religious institutions will keep us at least somewhat mindful that the calendar also includes holy days, but it is just as likely that our awareness of the shifts in the season will come from the coupons and advertisements included in our newspapers, which remind us that these are high-value shopping days. The thought that we are *commanded* to observe the sabbath is not, in most cases, the first imperative we consider when we mark our calendars.

Interpretation

Luke's description of Jesus reading scripture in the synagogue brings us a step closer to substantive issues relating to the question of scripture's authority. How did Jesus read scripture? What scripture(s) did Jesus regard as authoritative for his life? How did authoritative scriptures shape his life and ministry? We pastors and educators will frame these and other related questions with sophisticated nuances. Meanwhile, many of those to whom we minister will have taken their cue from a simple four-word question that fits on a rubberized bracelet, perhaps the modern analog of a religious icon: "What would Jesus do?" (aka, WWJD).

Luke reports "what Jesus did" on this particular occasion. He is given a scroll containing the words of Isaiah, and he finds (presumably chooses)[8] the place where the verses quoted from Isaiah occur. He quotes portions of two texts from the Septuagint of Isaiah 61:1–2 and 58:6, splicing the two together to form one "reading." We note that he not only rearranges the sequencing of these two texts but also (at least in Luke's version) adds to and subtracts from his source text. The italicized words below highlight the changes:

4:18 (Isa.61:1)   The Spirit of the Lord is upon me,
because he has anointed me
to bring good news to the poor
   [Luke omits: "*to bind up the brokenhearted.*"]
He has sent me to proclaim release to the captives
   [instead of: "*to proclaim liberty to the captives and release to the prisoners*"]
and recovery of sight to the blind,
   [not present in Isa.61:1; perhaps an allusion to Isa.35:5; 42:6–7]
to let the oppressed go free
   [*Isa.58:6, but omitting the rest of verse 6*]
4:19 (Isa.61:2)   to proclaim the year of the Lord's favor.
   [Luke omits: "*and the day of vengeance of our God; to comfort all who mourn*"]

Luke does not report that Jesus read the scripture in Hebrew nor that he translated it into Aramaic, though both these acts would likely have been customary (see Neh.8:8). Some form of exposition would also have typically accompanied the reading, and here Luke has Jesus speaking a brief but pregnant word: "Today this scripture has been fulfilled in your hearing" (4:21). When it comes to constructing a model for reading and hearing scripture as authoritative for the Christian community, surely this word is instructive. As with all such affirmations of scripture, however, this one invites and requires interpretation.

Jesus clearly recontextualizes the verses he quotes from Isaiah. If we assume that the scroll from which Jesus read contained the essence of the final form of the book, then we also know that in that context the one anointed with the "Spirit of the Lord" is an anonymous prophetic figure elusively described as God's "servant" (in the so-called "suffering servant" poems; Isaiah 42, 49, 50, and 52–53). Within the context of Deutero-Isaiah, this servant brings justice to Israelites who are languishing in Babylonian exile (42:1–4), is "a light to the nations" (49:6), and embodies the promise of God's presence by modeling the redemptive capacity of suffering (50:4–11; 52:12–53:13). In Luke's account, Jesus' threefold citation of the pronoun "me" has the function of equating his anointing by the Spirit with that previously given to the "servant" in Isaiah (cf. Luke 3:22; 4:1, 14). The Spirit now gives shape to Jesus' ministry in his own context and setting, which though centuries removed from that of Isaiah's "servant," sustains God's abiding promise of liberation and restoration to the poor, oppressed, and infirmed.

The recontextualization of Isaiah's scripture is also evident in the proclamation of the "year of the Lord's favor." The originating context for this proclamation is Leviticus 25, which contains the Priestly legislation concerning the Jubilee year of "release," when "you [the people of Israel] shall proclaim liberty throughout the land to all its inhabitants" (Lev.25:10). The "liberty" ("release," "freedom") envisioned is the promise that land that has been sold to pay off debts may be reclaimed (Lev.25:23–34), that those who have been forced to default on loans because of crop failure may work off their debts without paying interest (Lev.25:35–38), and that those who cannot work off their debts, and hence in effect have become slaves to their creditors, may be released from their servitude in the jubilee year. In Isaiah, the "servant" extends the promise of liberty encoded in the "year of the Lord's favor" to those broken and oppressed by exile. The audience and context are different, but the yearning for God's justice and mercy remains the same. In Luke 4, Jesus takes up the "old" promise and extends it to yet a different audience in another time and place. The "release" that God promises and that Jesus himself is now dramatically fulfilling is not limited to a *year* on a priestly calculated calendar; it is *an era* of peace and justice inaugurated by the radically new in-breaking of the "kingdom of God" (Luke 4:43). Its reality is manifest, according to Luke's gospel, in the promise of redemption that Jesus extends to all people, regardless of their social, economic, or religious status. For a preview of this ministry, we need look no further than the pericopes immediately following this one in Luke 4, which describe Jesus teaching and healing in Capernaum (4:31–44).[9]

Luke's description of Jesus' recontextualization of scripture invites two observations. First, we should note that the same scripture has authority in different settings and in more than one way. We may conceptualize this by considering the difference between scripture's *kerygmatic* and *confessional* functions.[10] *Kerygma* refers in the first instance to scripture's "preaching" or "proclamation" of some irreducible faith-assertion about the *nature of God*. The kerygma in I John 4:16, for example, is that "God is love." The *confessional* aspect of scripture refers to various responses that one may offer to faith-assertions about who God is. For example, I John 4:16 is completed with the confessional statement that 'Those who say, 'I love God', and hate their brothers or sisters, are liars" (I John 4:20). There is one asserted truth—"God is love"—but multiple possible confessional responses, e.g., "I choose to love as God loves" or "I choose, irrespective of what God may do, to hate others." By analogy, we may extend this distinction to Luke 4. In quoting from Isaiah 61 and 58, Jesus endorses a particular kerygma, namely, wherever God is present, there is the promise of redemption and restoration. Jesus' own confessional response is a commitment to embody this truth about God in the way he lives. Others may decide to respond differently (see, for example, Luke 4:28–29), in which case it is the kergyma that judges the confession, not vice versa. When it comes to evaluating the authority of scripture, scripture itself insists that "the kerygmatic has priority over the confessional."[11]

Second, Luke's description of how Jesus reads and modifies Isaiah invites us to understand that scripture requires ongoing interpretation. Long after history designates ancient texts as sacred scripture, successive generations of readers must decide if and how scripture's canonical truths have relevance for a contemporary world. Contrary to what we may assume, scriptural truths are seldom, if ever, simple, assured, or uncontested. On this point, Robert Alter's observations are cogent. In his view, scripture provides a "lexicon for imagining" how we might live with or against its semantic sweep. Even when we concede scriptural status to an ancient text, we have to choose whether we will embrace its claims about God and life in relation to God or resist them. Scripture's imperative does not close or finalize our search for truth; instead, it opens it up and keeps it alive with the promise of new possibilities. These new possibilities are nowhere more inviting than when the New Testament cites the Old, as in Luke 4, for this engagement of the "old" with the "new" generates, Alter suggests, a "culture of exegesis"—both within and beyond the Bible[12]—that survives to this day. Within this culture, Alter argues, every time a word from scripture is read, whether in ancient Nazareth or modern Chicago, those who hear are summoned to an "imaginative allegiance" to truths that are at once both "ungraspable" and "continually "mesmerizing."[13]

"Good news to the poor": An ethical criterion for Biblical authority

What should we make of Luke's report that Jesus "found the place" where these particular verses from Isaiah are written? I am struck by the fact that of all the scriptures Jesus might have read on this sabbath day, he chose ones that accent the ethical imperative to release persons from various forms of bondage—spiritual, economic, political, and physical. Such an emphasis is of course particularly congenial to Luke, whose gospel gives special attention to Jesus' compassion for the broken and bruised, a radically inclusive category of persons that includes Jews and Samaritans, men and women, rich and poor, those whom society regards as reputable and those deemed beyond or beneath society's concern. Perhaps this emphasis can be attributed to tradition's identification of Luke as not only a companion of Paul but also as a "beloved physician" (cf. Col.4:14; II Tim.4:11). Eusebius (fourth century), for example, describes Luke as one who had expertise in the "art of curing souls." For whatever reason, Luke is more precise than the other gospel writers in his descriptions of the illnesses and afflictions that rob healthy people of life and reduce them to outcasts in a world that readily assumes all suffering is a punishment for sin. In Luke's view, Jesus has come into the world to teach, preach, and demonstrate the good news that God cares for all such persons.

In thinking about what Luke's report of Jesus reading scripture in Nazareth might contribute to a contemporary model for biblical authority, I have found Gerd Theissen's work particularly instructive.[14] In *Biblical Faith: An Evolutionary Approach* (1988), Theissen argues that from time to time, the human race shows itself capable of what he calls an "evolution against evolution." At such times, the inherent selfishness of genetic and biological (and even cultural) development, which adheres to the Darwinian principle of the "survival of the fittest," goes into reverse. Mutations and recombinations mysteriously conspire against the process of selection to produce something new, the altruistic concern to protect and care for the weakest among us. Theissen sees this happening in two distinct phases of human religious history: in the increasingly monotheistic faith of ancient Israel, which grounds the meaning of life in one and only one God, the ultimate source and sustainer of everything in the cosmos; and in the life, teaching, and death of Jesus of Nazareth, who reveals and exemplifies the most complete "adaptation to the reality of God"[15] history has ever witnessed.

In a recent publication, *The Bible and Contemporary Culture* (2007), Theissen extends this argument by focusing on how these two moments in history have indelibly inscribed contemporary culture. A brief excerpt from his comments on "Why Any Educated Person Should Know the Bible" introduces the salient aspects of the larger discussion. From the scriptures of the ancient Israelites, we receive:

- an "*image of humanity* that ascribes to each individual, made in the image of God, an inviolable dignity";
- an "impressive *mandative ethics*, by making the law of God—still alive today in the Decalogue and the command to love one's neighbor—independent of all human authorities";
- a "*vision of history* that makes human beings responsible for the course of events, but also drives them to repent and change when it is necessary to turn away from a disastrous past"; and
- an "*understanding of God* that saw God as a focus of infinite ethical energy."[16]

Jesus teaches and lives in accord with each of these fundamental Jewish beliefs, even as he shapes them in distinctive ways. But Theissen calls attention especially to the way in which Jesus incarnates "God's brilliant ethical energy," an energy that "manifests itself as a glowing fire of love, which can blaze into the flames of hell if opposed."[17] In the way Jesus lived and died, we see the distillation of the mandative ethics of a God who is on the side of the downtrodden rather than their oppressors. It is the imperative of the God who was in Jesus, the one and same God who seeks to bring a new, supranatural order of justice and peace out of the natural laws of selection that spell death, not life, for the weak and powerless. In sum, Theissen argues, we see in ancient Israel and in primitive Christianity two places in history where religion takes a decisive turn, away from supporting an ethos in which "only the strong survive," toward a fundamentally new ethos committed to solidarity with the weak and healing for the wounded.

"And he rolled up the scroll, gave it back to the attendant...they got up, drove him out of town..."

I am attempting to make a case that the authority of scripture in the modern world may be better located in the moral and ethical behavior it elicits from its readers than in the knowledge, beliefs, or doctrines that its readers profess. We may believe and promulgate biblical truths as witness to ultimate reality; but this alone will not validate them for anyone who does not already agree with us. Theissen makes the point as follows:

> [A]s we know only too well, the functionality of an ethos does not validate it. No matter how many people are convinced that they should conform to a certain set of rules, the result is not normative force but merely social pressure to conform. The fundamental principle remains: *imperatives do not follow from facts*. Standards accepted by many are not necessarily norms. It is therefore a huge leap from the observation that a particular ethos has proved its worth and functionality to personal commitment to that ethos. Such a commitment means *inward affirmation*. It means adherence to it amid all the conflicts of life, *practicing it in spite of all the detriments it brings, readiness to sacrifice one's life rather than one's convictions*.[18]

Here again, I believe Luke's description of Jesus reading scripture is instructive...and sobering. He reports that on first hearing Jesus' words, "everyone was giving testimony (imperfect tense) about him; they were amazed at the words about God's grace (reading an objective genitive here) that came from his mouth" (4:22). Upon further reflection, however, presumably after they realized that the good news they believed extended only to them was not theirs to control, "they were filled with rage" and "drove him out of the town" (4:29). At the risk of over interpreting, I venture this observation. It is not the opening of the scroll, the reading of its words, or the verbal affirmation of its truths that validates its authority. Only when the scroll is closed, when words proclaimed as scripture and affirmed by belief are embodied in palpable behavior, can convictions about the "authority of scripture" exert a demonstrable claim on our lives. The last word in this particular pericope from Luke, therefore, offers both a judgment and a promise. Even as those who heard his words were "giving testimony" to truth they were unwilling to act upon, Jesus was "going on" (*eporeueto*; 4:30)...to other proclamations of the truth about God, to other demonstrations of this truth's power to transform lives, and to other people in different times and places who would have opportunity to hear and respond differently (cf. Luke 4:31–44). It is this "going on" witness to scripture's authority, I suggest, that compels us to gather round this table today.

"So Now...What Does the Lord Your God Require of You?" (Deut.10:12; cf. Mic.6:8)
"What Then Should We Do?" (Luke 3:10, 12, 14)

These questions set the table for concluding this paper. The first comes from the scripture we know as the Old Testament. It is anchored in Moses' final sermon to those who had received the Torah at Sinai and were now being prompted to consider how they would live out its truths in the new world of Canaan (Deut.10:12). The question is sustained in the preaching of the prophet Micah, who insists that the same Torah presents the same question to those in eighth century Jerusalem, who may be tempted to believe that they no longer need to heed the Torah's imperative "to do justice and to love kindness." The second citation, which comes from Luke, reminds us that "old" Torah truths linger in history; long after the times and places that first defined them as important, they beckon responses that remain consequential.

Luke's recapitulation of the question occurs in a pericope that precedes the one in chapter 4 on which I have been focused. He reports that when the crowds came to John the Baptist requesting "a baptism of repentance for the forgiveness of sins," John responded by saying that before he could do what they asked, they must first "bear fruits worthy of repentance" (Luke 3:3, 7; cf.6:43–4; 13:6–9). The diverse crowd responds, in turn, with a question, three times repeated: "What should we do?" (Luke 3:10, 12, 14). John's answer is Luke's version of the Torah's mandative ethics, the behavior required by repentance:

> [To "the crowds"] Whoever has two coats must share with anyone who has none; and whoever has food must do likewise...
>
> [To the tax collectors] Collect no more than the amount prescribed for you...
>
> [To the "soldiers"] Do not extort money from anyone by threats or false accusation, and be satisfied with your own wages. (Luke 3:11, 13, 14)

"The fruits of repentance." What does this mean? I take a cue once again from Theissen, who notes that in Matthew's account of the Sermon on the Mount, Jesus uses similar language to explicate the one criterion that defines all those who would be Jesus' disciples: "you shall know them *by their fruits*" (Matt.7:16. 20). The point of this Matthean metaphor, I believe, is that neither *knowledge* of the scriptures nor *belief* about God will count for very much in the final judgment. The one criterion for deciding who has truly done the will of God will be the fruit produced by those rooted in the radical ethic of God's commandment to love others. The quintessential expression of this ethic, rooted as Matthew insists in the "law and the prophets" (the phrase Matthew uses both to frame and summarize Jesus' teaching; 5:17; 22:40), is the so-called Golden Rule: "In everything you do, do to others as you would have them to do you" (7:12; cf. Luke 6:31).

Theissen applies this "by their fruit" criterion in support of the following proposal:

> Religions, I believe, should be approached in two ways. First they should be known and judged *ethically*, "by their fruits" (Matt.7:16, 20); second, they must be respected *religiously* for their beliefs, even if these appear alien.[19]

It is clear that Theissen regards both the ethical (moral conduct) and the religious (beliefs) aspects of religions as important criteria for assessing their contribution to the modern world. Nonetheless, his sequencing of these two criteria hints that the ethical component has priority. Why might this be so? Theissen's answer is closely argued, and I cannot do it justice in the limitations of this paper. We can however gain a toehold on its essentials by turning to his invitation to consider an imaginary scene:

> Let us imagine that at the end of the ages the "Heavenly Academy of Sciences" is charged to select from all books and traditions whatever will be deemed true for all eternity. If we believe that the Bible in its core belongs to this "eternal canon," we affirm it as Holy Scripture. There is no reason that this canon cannot include texts from other religions. We do not know which they

might be. We should remain open to the possibility that we would find many texts from other religions in this canon, but also the possibility that it might not include the whole of the Bible! One criterion used by these heavenly scholars—perhaps not the only one—would be the extent to which the texts are committed to an anti-Darwinian spirit.[20]

Let me try to "unpack" the argumentation that foregrounds Theissen's invitation to consider this hypothetical scenario.

- In the modern world, the context within which all religions must vie for a hearing is the tension between scientific thought and faith.[21] Scientific statements privilege the *hypothetical* (*if* X can be empirically verified, *then* Y is the result); faith statements privilege unconditional affirmations that are true, regardless of empirical data (X is true, even if the "facts" may not support it). Scientific thought is always subject to falsification and thus can and must be corrected or modified as the facts require; faith assertions, while not impervious to changing empirical data, are tuned to transcendent certainties that resist mere "facts." Scientific thought not only invites and requires debate about alternative possibilities, which happily promote disagreement and dissension. Faith promulgations seek consensus, not dissent; they aim at conformity to authoritative truths that unite rather than divide. Theissen's first sentence in the citation above, which cedes the final say in this debate to the "Heavenly Academy of *Sciences*" invites us to ponder carefully the strengths and weaknesses of the religious argument in a world where competing truths vie for commitment.
- In a modern, pluralistic society, Theissen argues, Judaeo-Christian assertions about God and humankind do not have unquestioned authority. Christians and Jews may, indeed must, bear witness to the transcendent truths by which they live. But they must know that virtually every testimony buttressed by faith convictions stands to be cross-examined by faithful witnesses from other religions who have different convictions about ultimate truths. When it comes to ultimate reality, Theissen contends, all religions "must be respected religiously for their beliefs, even if they appear alien" to those who do not agree with them. If there were a day of final judgment before a "Heavenly Academy of Sciences," where decisions will be made about what is true "for all eternity," then we may

imagine that religious beliefs will call attention to the differences that separate one religion's claims to superiority from another. Such a judgment is not unimportant; indeed, the sad truth may be that our "hermeneutical civil war[s] over the interpretation of texts"[22] may require it. But what if we imagine that the most important criterion for deciding what is "eternally true" is the extent to which the texts by which we live commit us to an "anti-Darwinian spirit"? That is, what if the final judgment on the authority of any sacred text—the Bible, the Qur'an, the Tipitaka, the Bhagavad-Gita—is its demonstrable capacity to transform the way those who *confess* its truths *live*? What if the final criterion is obedience to a "mandative ethic," which transcends all other authorities, to live in ways that make life possible for the weakest among us?

If we were to concede that the final decision on the authority of the Bible depends not on the creeds or confessions it inspires but instead on the ethical behavior it *authorizes*[23] and empowers, *then* how would the Bible fare in Theissen's imaginary scene in the "Heavenly Academy of Sciences"? I am struck by the parallel between the hypothetical assessment by "heavenly scholars" in Theissens's imaginary end-of-time scenario and the last judgment envisioned by the Bible itself.

Of the Gospel writers, only Matthew gives us any details about this "last judgment." Following a long series of six parables about what it means to live responsibly so as to be ready for the coming of the Son of Man (Matt.24:32–25:30), Matthew invites us to consider this scene:

> When the Son of Man comes in his glory, and all the angels with him, he will sit on the throne of his glory. All the nations will be gathered before him, and he will separate people from one another as a shepherd separates the sheep from the goats, and he will put the sheep at his right hand and the goats at the left. Then the king will say to those at his right hand, "Come, you that are blessed by my Father, inherit the kingdom prepared for you from the foundation of the world; for I was hungry and you gave me food, I was thirsty and you gave me something to drink, I was a stranger and you welcomed me, I was naked and you gave me clothing, I was sick and you took care of me, I was in prison and you visited me." Then the righteous will answer him, "Lord, when was it that we saw you hungry and gave you food, or thirsty and

gave you something to drink? And when was it that we saw you a stranger and welcomed you, or naked and gave you clothing? And when was it that we saw you sick or in prison and visited you?" And the king will answer them, "Truly I tell you, just as you did it to the least of these who are members of my family, you did it to me."

Then he will say to those at his left hand, "You that are accursed, depart from me into the eternal fire prepared for the devil and his angels; for I was hungry and you gave me no food, I was thirsty and you gave me nothing to drink, I was a stranger and you did not welcome me, naked and you did not give me clothing, sick and in prison and you did not visit me." Then they also will answer, "Lord, when was it that we saw you hungry or thirsty or a stranger or naked or sick or in prison, and did not take care of you?" Then he will answer them, "Truly I tell you, just as you did not do it to one of the least of these, you did not do it to me." And these will go away into eternal punishment, but the righteous into life. (Matt.25:31–46)

Matthew says nothing about belief, creeds, or confessions. Instead, the gospel in this Gospel is that the only thing that matters on the Day of Judgment is whether we have acted with loving care for needy people. According to Matthew, the one and only decisive criterion for entering the kingdom of God are *deeds* of love and mercy that feed the hungry, give drink to the thirsty, clothe the naked, and offer community and communion to strangers who have no place to call home.

Theissen is reaching for a model for reading the Bible in "interconfessional dialogue" with other religions. His agenda is related to but not exactly the same as ours. Nevertheless, his wonderment about the usefulness of an ethical criterion for the authority of scripture is instructive, and may in fact seed the discussions we will pursue. Would adherence to an ethical criterion for the authority of sacred scriptures enable all human beings, whatever their religious convictions, to live more meaningfully, more fully, more wholly, in a world that too often privileges only the strongest among us? Theissen frames the question and proposes an answer along the following lines.

For relationships between human beings all are subject to the same ethical criteria; for relationship to transcendence, all respect their distinguishing religious characteristics. Could religions live side by side in "reconciled diversity" in this manner? *This formula would not end the controversy over truth, but the debate would obey certain rules*—which of course would have to be redefined repeatedly.[24]

If scripture has the power to shape and constrain human beings for relationships that conform to transcendent truths, then its suasion will likely come more from the ways in which we live our lives than from ecclesiastical debates over the truth of this or that confession about God. If it is obedience to an ethic for life that does justice to God (or to "ultimate reality"), then the old words of Isaiah, proclaimed anew by Jesus of Nazareth, bear witness to the abiding authority of scripture in the modern world, which, of course, as Theissen reminds us, has to be repeatedly redefined.

Notes

1. Green, William Scott, "Levitical Religion," in *Judaism from Moses to Muhammad: An Interpretation. Turning Points and Focal Points*, eds., Jacob Neusner, William Scott Green, and Alan J. Avery Peck (The Brill Library of Reference; Leiden, Boston: Brill, 2005), 3.
2. Ibid., 9.
3. Ibid. The internal reference to Mary Douglas is from *Leviticus as Literature* (Oxford: Oxford University Press, 1993), 230.
4. Note the recent spate of best-selling books—from scientists and philosophers—which argue that religion is a scourge on society, e.g., Dawkins, R., *The God Delusion* (New York: Houghton Mifflin, 2006); Dennett, D., *Breaking the Spell: Religion as a Natural Phenomenon* (New York: Allen Lane, 2006); and Harris, S., *The End of Faith: Religion, Terror, and the Future of Reason* (New York: W. W. Norton, 2005).
5. My formulation of this issue draws upon the cogent observations of Gerd Theissen concerning "The Bible in Dialogue with a Pluralistic World," in *The Bible and Contemporary Culture* (Minneapolis: Fortress, 2007), 142–9.
6. Other common terms for synagogue, such as "house of prayer" and "house of learning/inquiry/study" suggest a similar understanding.
7. Most of the archeological evidence for synagogues in the Galilee region comes from the late first to the fourth centuries CE, which suggests that the descriptions found in Luke and the New Testament reflect the role of the synagogue at the time of the authors.
8. We may be reasonably confident that by the first century there was a fixed triennial cycle of readings from the Torah. The evidence for fixed readings from the Prophets at this time is however less clear. Texts were probably chosen because they contained thematic or linguistic affinities with the readings from the Torah. By describing Jesus as "finding"

these texts particular texts from Isaiah, Luke hints that Jesus was making an intentional choice.

9. By incorporating the line from Isa 58:6—"to let the oppressed go free" or "to send the oppressed away in release"—Luke accents the promise of "release." The term (*apehesis*) is elsewhere used in Luke only for the forgiveness of sins (e.g., 1:77; 3:3; 24:47), but here Luke seems to be saying that Jesus understands that forgiveness of sin, no less than liberation from economic, physical, or political affliction, is a form of liberation from bondage.

10. On this distinction, see further, Jodock, D., *The Church's Bible: Its Contemporary Authority* (Minneapolis: Fortress, 1989), 120–5.

11. Ibid., 138.

12. Alter, R., *Canon and Creativity: Modern Writing and the Authority of Scripture* (New Haven, CT: Yale University Press, 2000). As the title indicates, Alter's focus is on the potency of scripture for modern writers (specifically Franz Kafka, Haim Nahman Bailik, and James Joyce), whose writings bear witness to the enduring importance of biblical images for their own urgent concerns.

13. Ibid., 11, 15–6, 77.

14. See especially, *Biblical Faith: An Evolutionary Approach* (Philadelphia: Fortress, 1985); *The Bible and Contemporary Culture* (Minneapolis: Fortress, 2007).

15. Theissen, Gerd, *Biblical Faith*, 83.

16. Theissen, Gerd, *The Bible and Contemporary Culture*, 11.

17. Ibid., 38.

18. Ibid., 84 (emphasis added).

19. *The Bible and Contemporary Culture*, 137.

20. Ibid., 140.

21. See, Theissen, *Biblical Faith*, 3–8.

22. Theissen, Gerd, *The Bible and Contemporary Culture*, 142.

23. On the use of the word "authorize" as a way of conceptualizing biblical authority, see the seminal work of Kelsey, D., *The Uses of Scripture in Recent Theology* (Philadelphia and London: SCM Press, 1975), and its application by, for example, Brueggemann, W., "Biblical Authority in the Post-Critical Period," ABD V, 1049–56.

24. Ibid., 140 (emphasis added).

REVERENCE DESPITE REJECTION
The Paradox of Early Christian Views of Biblical Authority

Adam Gregerman

Introduction

Among the different forms of inter-religious dialogue, Jewish-Christian dialogue is unique in that both sides affirm the authority of the Hebrew Bible.[1] Since the triumph of the "orthodox" Christian argument in the first few centuries CE for retaining the Bible as sacred Scripture over Marcionite and gnostic rejection, the dominant Christian position has been that the Bible is a Christian holy book alongside the writings eventually gathered in the New Testament.[2] As we will see, the implications of this vary, but in general terms Jews and Christians alike revere and seek guidance from this text. Because of this shared source, Jewish-Christian dialogue can be especially rich, as participants consider the diverse ways that the text has been interpreted over time.

Despite much that is similar in Jewish and Christian traditions, however, disagreements about the authority of the Bible are especially common. This is not surprising, for claims about authority can reflect diverse understandings of the nature of this authority. They can encompass, for example, affirmations about authorship, the reliability of the text (e.g., historically or doctrinally), or requirements to perform or refrain from specific actions.[3] This last topic—the binding status of the many biblical commandments in religious life—is, and long has been, especially contentious between Jews and Christians, and it is this that I want to investigate. It arose repeatedly in the recent colloquia on "The Scandal of Particularity," and in my experience surfaces often in dialogue between Jews and Christians. Specifically, I want to focus on Christian rejection of many of the biblical commandments. Commandments on circumcision, food, purity, Sabbath and holidays—these and others, despite the biblical requirements, were dropped by many in the early church, a position largely followed thereafter. In simplest terms, then, how do Christians affirm the authority of the Hebrew Bible while dispensing with observance of (some of) the commandments?

My paper is offered as a contribution to greater clarity and understanding of seminal early Christian writings on biblical authority. In my experiences Jews have often struggled to understand this seeming incongruity in Christian thought: praise of faithfulness to the Bible sits uneasily alongside Christian rejection of some or most of the commands of the Bible.[4] A survey of works by three foundational figures in the early church will reveal both distinctive ideas of each and also important commonalities. I consider how they defend this view of biblical authority, which, despite minor variations, is generally shared by all of them. I begin by looking at the letters of Paul, which contain claims taken up by nearly all later interpreters. I then turn to two of the most important later writers, Irenaeus from the second century and Origen from the third.[5] While other Christians both before and after offer their own interpretations, these three writers together provide some of the most influential responses to this vital issue.

Despite my commitment to improved Jewish-Christian relations, I do not minimize what I, as a Jew, perceive to be eisegetical or radical about some of these views. I might better say that *because* of my commitment to improved Jewish-Christian relations, it is all the more important to understand these writers' views, for their remarkable influence on Christian thought and obvious sophistication make them essential contributors to a topic of immense and continuing importance. There is something scandalous in many religious claims, those of both Jews and Christians, for others with different assumptions, contexts, and especially goals. This is true regarding biblical authority and the status of the commandments, as much as anywhere else. Though most Jews know *that* Christians' views differ dramatically, I hope a careful delineation of *how* some reached these views will clarify a complex issue.

Paul

Paul offers some of the most provocative and influential Christian discussions of the authority of the Hebrew Bible. He treats the topic extensively, because it complicates his efforts to bring Gentiles into an originally all-Jewish, Law-observant religious movement without requiring observance of the biblical commandments. This provoked opposition from prominent Jewish Christians, and his letters are intensely polemical.[6] Paul often emphasizes what divides him from his opponents regarding his views on the Law, though one should not lose sight of what unites them. Paul, like Jesus and his followers, including Paul's opponents, was a Jew who affirmed the divine authorship of the Hebrew Bible, which alone was their sacred scripture.[7] It is essential for understanding God's interactions with and plans for humanity, and for its prophetic foreshadowing of the events of Jesus' life and of the church. Disagreements in the early church that are apparent in many New Testament texts should not overshadow this. Of course, the authority of the Hebrew Bible is understood in diverse ways, but Paul shares a reverence for and reliance on the text, which profoundly shapes his own thinking. Explicit biblical quotations, innumerable allusions, traditional categories of biblical thought (e.g., holiness, worship, covenant, faith), and, most important for our purposes, a fundamental affirmation that religious knowledge is derived above all from the Bible: all of these characterize Paul's writings.

While there is great complexity and perhaps confusion in his views (see below), we should note a few ways he affirms the Bible's authority. The Bible reveals God's will, and the divine plan of salvation (Rom 1:2, 17). Historical events—above all Jesus' resurrection—can only be understood by reference to its ancient promises (1 Cor 15:3-4). He appeals to the Bible to legitimate unexpected developments, for example, the influx of Gentiles into an originally all-Jewish religious movement (Gal 3:8; Rom 9:6-33). In this regard, the Bible authorizes decisions of church leaders, for missionizing, worship, communal organization, etc., and is a trustworthy source of guidance in all areas of religious life. Biblical commandments are applied to the contemporary community (Rom 15:4; 1 Cor 9:9-14). Believers should strive to "fulfill" them, for example, through love of neighbor (Gal 5:14) and avoidance of theft and adultery (Rom 13:8-10).[8]

Paul, like other ancient interpreters, sometimes blithely ignores the original meaning or context of a biblical text in order to find ways of linking the Bible to Jesus or the needs of his own community. Nonetheless, he insists that he is only being faithful to the Bible. This is important, he says, for he would not contradict this authoritative text (Rom 3:31). Even in his most fanciful interpretations, in places of undeniable eisegesis, in passages where he contradicts the plain sense of the original text, he does not question the authority of the text. Rather, he argues that he is faithful to it and properly understands it, even at the very moment he rejects (some of) the commandments.[9]

It is precisely on this point, however, that his views get murky and, for many Jews, confusing, for his affirmation of the authority of the Bible is joined to an almost violent opposition to the requirement to observe its commandments. His view of authority is therefore limited, for he denies that the text has any binding force on believers' religious practices. He famously sets up an antithesis between faith in Jesus and observance of the commandments (Gal 2:16; Phil 3:9). One's righteousness depends entirely on assent to a theological conviction about Jesus' status before God (Rom 10:9). Therefore, his followers must resist the demands of other Jewish Christian preachers who, like many non-Christian Jews, insisted that Gentiles could not be equal members of religious communities without observing the commandments (Gal 3:1-4:31; Phil 3:2-4:1). Faced with rivals' demands that believers be circumcised and avoid non-kosher foods, for example, Paul angrily denounces the Bible and its many laws, and wishes that those who argue that its requirements are binding should "castrate themselves" (Gal 5:12). Statements of reverence for the text noted earlier sit uneasily alongside these very different ideas.

Scholars have long debated his views on this issue,[10] though it is possible to explain them generally as a reflection of the practical needs of his missionary work among Gentiles.[11] Actually, the extent of his opposition to the Law is quite limited, for he almost always has in mind the rituals that separate Jews from Gentiles, such as those noted above. In his work founding and leading churches, he bristled at religious (and ethnic and social) boundaries, for believers composed one unified community of those who affirmed Jesus as Lord. Distinctions between Jews and Gentiles (at meals, worship, etc.) were antithetical to their complete equality before God (Gal 3:28). Observance of the biblical commands might divide a church into factions.

His rejection of biblical authority in this regard fundamentally reflects his overriding desire to unify a diverse community in an unprecedented and highly controversial way. Without oversimplifying his views, it is clear that his responsibilities as leader of small, mostly Gentile religious communities consistently prompt his opposition to anything that gets in the way of that which was most important: "to proclaim [Jesus] among the Gentiles" (Gal 1:16; cf. 1 Cor 1:23; 2:2). He therefore denied the Bible's authority, perhaps even for Jews as well.[12] Given the harshness of his critique and zealous advocacy of his positions, it is not easy to disentangle precisely his views, though one might also argue he referred only to Gentiles.[13] However, his most polemical statements against the binding authority of the Bible were ultimately influential for later Christians, who adapted his basic claims to their own unique circumstances.

Irenaeus
Irenaeus of Lyon was a profound thinker on issues of intense concern in the early church. Among his many contributions is his discussion of biblical authority in Against Heresies (late 2nd C). This is a response to gnostic Christians who denied that the God of Israel is also the God of Jesus. Because the Bible's author was a deity they rejected as inconsistent and cruel, they also rejected the text. It had no authority as sacred scripture to shape their religious beliefs or enjoin any specific behaviors. In response, Irenaeus extensively defends the Bible. Specifically, he defends the "orthodox" decision to retain it as a sacred Christian text while also explaining how it should be read and how its many laws are to be understood, or more precisely, why many did not need to be followed by Christians. His main claims are familiar from our discussion of Paul's, though his circumstances differ greatly (e.g., Jewish Christianity is not a threat). However, his arguments are more systematic and complex, and his conclusions more explicit and far-reaching.[14]

Above all, the Bible derives it authority from its divine authorship. The God worshipped by Christians is the God responsible for the Bible (4:36:5). Irenaeus praises the Bible as "indeed perfect, since [its verses] were spoken by the Word of God" (2:28:2). He disputes gnostic accusations that it is the revelation of a lesser or evil deity, arguing that it reveals the one God to humanity. Jesus' frequent appeals to the Bible demonstrate that he worshipped no other deity and trusted no other text (3:12:12, 15). It is a sure guide to religious life, teaching love of God and of one's neighbor. These are the greatest demands, binding on all (4:12:2-3).

The Bible's prophetic sections are equally important. They "prepares [humans] for the coming of Christ" (4:12:1). For Irenaeus, who wants to refute those who deny any special status to the Bible, the prophetic foreshadowings of Jesus prove that the Bible is sacred and holy, and a divine revelation (4:26:1; 4:33:10). Its authority in this regard lies in its trustworthiness, for it provides vital information about Christ that Irenaeus' opponents disregard. The believer's faith is only established when the Bible is relied upon (4:32:2). It is therefore wrong to neglect or ignore it, for it reveals fundamental truths about God and Christ (4:34:5). Its divine authorship guarantees its veracity (the text is trustworthy) and its relevance (it points forward to Jesus and the Church).

However, when addressing the Bible's detailed moral and ritual laws, he is far less positive about the authority of the text to command specific behaviors. He oscillates between different, perhaps contradictory statements. This might be expected, for despite his strong endorsement of the Bible as an authoritative source for Christian belief and practice, he believes that almost no specific biblical commandments are actually binding (apart from the Decalogue; see below) (4:4:2). There is an unavoidable tension in this position, for, as we have seen, he has high praise for the Bible. Against his gnostic opponents, he vigorously denies that Christians do not recognize the binding authority of the Bible.

On the one hand, Irenaeus can be surprisingly reluctant to endorse openly the abrogation of any of the commandments. Jesus, he says, did not instruct his disciples to break the laws, but only to be more rigorous in observing them. Nothing Jesus taught was "opposed to the Law" (4:13:1; cf. 4:8:3). His healing on the Sabbath, for example, was not against the Law, but only against some Jews' interpretations of the Law.[15] On the other hand, Irenaeus unambiguously rejects the binding authority of the Bible for any part of the Law besides the Decalogue. This short code alone was God's original revelation, the only part of the Law that must be followed by Christians (4:15:1; 4:16:5).[16] He supports this by quoting the statement that follows the Decalogue in Deuteronomy

5:22—"These words the Lord spoke…and he added no more"—to argue that these ten commandments *alone* were the content of God's original message. Only after the sin of the golden calf did Moses give them additional rules, which are not authoritative and binding commandments of God. While his chronology is imprecise (there are many commandments between the revelation of the Decalogue in Exod 20 and the building of the golden calf in Exod 32), he wants to establish a separation between those laws that are binding on Christians and those that are binding only on Jews.

He justifies the abrogation of biblical commandments with a few arguments. The upright behavior of the heroes of Genesis, who lived before the giving of the Law, proves that it is possible to be righteous apart from the Law. Even though living before Moses, they had the Decalogue's "natural" precepts written on their hearts (4:13-16). The other biblical laws have a lesser, non-binding status, and were given by God to the Jews alone. With these laws, God sought to check their proclivity for sin and temporarily educate them for righteousness (4:15:1-2). While this need not necessarily undermine the binding status of the Bible, practically Irenaeus circumscribes the demands for obedience to one people, the Jews, and one period of time, between Moses and Jesus. Note as well that he has practical concerns with the emergence of a Gentile church for which these commandments were an unacceptable imposition. Even the demand that one not work on the Sabbath, from the Decalogue itself, is effectively abolised (4:8:2-3), for this had been seen, already before Irenaeus, as an onerous and unacceptable imposition.[17] Though Irenaeus was not a missionary defending Jew-Gentile equality like Paul, Irenaeus likewise emphasizes the universality of Christian salvation and interprets the Bible so as to legitimate Gentile inclusion (4:22:2; 4:24:1-2).

Irenaeus is delicately balancing competing interests. He vigorously defends the Bible, for its role foreshadowing Jesus, its few eternally binding precepts, and most importantly, its divine authorship. At the same time, he limits its authority severely. As a leader of an increasingly Gentile church, without any interest in convincing Jews of his claims, the requirements of the Law are presented as unacceptable and indeed irrelevant. Though he insists that Christians better fulfill the Law than the Jews, sometimes even literally, his affirmation of biblical authority is seldom applied to actual observance.[18] His concern to refute the gnostics provides the necessary context for his claims. Because of their intense hostility to the Law, he was understandably reluctant to openly break with the Law, though his notion of authority is one to which no Jew likely would assent.

Origen

Origen, writing in the middle of the third century from Alexandria and Caesarea, like Irenaeus and Paul walks a fine line between defense of the Bible as a sacred and authoritative religious text, and opposition to Christian observance of its many commandments. A threat that Paul faced—counter-missionaries who demanded that Gentile believers observe Jewish law—has mostly became irrelevant with the waning of Jewish Christianity by his time. The gnostic threat, like that faced by Irenaeus, had not disappeared, prompting Origen's zealous defense of biblical authority, though his responses are somewhat different. They reflect his deep commitment to allegorical interpretation of the Bible and unconventional ideas about the Law.

Like Paul and Irenaeus, Origen absolutely affirms that the Hebrew Bible is the work of the one God, the God of Israel who is also the God of Jesus (Hom. on Numbers 5:59). Especially important to Origen is the notion of divine authorship (Celsus 3:3; 5:60; First Principles 1:3:1). On this claim he is uncompromising, stressing that "not a single dot [of the Bible] is devoid of the wisdom of God."[19] Though influenced by Greco-Roman philosophy, Origen insists that all religious truth is found within this one book. Surprisingly for a Gentile Christian, he sometimes grants the Bible binding authority for specific behavior. Christians are to refrain from work on the Sabbath (Hom. on Num 23:4). They are not to eat meat that still has blood in it (Celsus 8:30). Likewise, the Bible's eternal commands, such as the command to honor one's parents, are to be followed. The Bible's historical reliability is undisputed when it refers to certain actual events in the past, such as Abraham's burial in Hebron or the building of Solomon's Temple.[20] These parallel some views we have seen earlier, but Origen occasionally is much more accepting of the Bible's authority for specific ritual acts.

As noted, he can speak positively about the Bible as a legally authoritative code, even when discussing Jewish observance. Unlike most other early Christians, who harshly denigrated it, he is surprisingly accepting of the Jews' adherence to at least some commandments when it was suitable for them to do so (e.g., on criminal justice and war, when they had political power; Celsus 7:25). When defending Jews against the pagan Celsus' condemnation, he can identify some positive value in the requirements, though they were a temporary accommodation by God for the Jews. There is here a parallel to earlier Christians' claims that the authority of the Bible was time-limited, though prominent in Origen is the reliance on historical events to buttress this argument, above all the destruction of the Jerusalem Temple in 70 CE. He links this one event, which immediately prevented the observance of many biblical commandments such as sacrifice, with a broader criticism of biblical authority for Christians (Celsus 4:22; 7:26). Because these could no longer be done, God was signaling that the authority of the Bible, at least as the Jews understood it, had changed.[21]

It is when we turn to Origen's embrace of allegory that we recognize the most prominent influence on Origen's views of biblical authority. He argues that verses in the Bible, despite their obvious meaning, point beyond themselves to something else. This can be an event in Jesus' life or the early church, or the text can address an issue of concern in the contemporary church. This not only affects how he interprets individual verses of Scripture, it also shapes his entire perspective on the status and meaning of the Bible as a text with a hidden meaning. This meaning may be distant from what Jews or others identify as the plain sense of the text (and thereby unacceptable and even baffling to them), but this method nonetheless reveals a dedication to the Bible even when seeming to reject it.

Allegory was practiced by ancient Jewish exegetes, and Origen was influenced by them.[22] A comparison, however, makes clear how different Origen's use of allegory is, and how this sharply affects his views of biblical authority. The most prominent example is the first century Jew Philo (whose work Origen knew), who often downplays the literal sense of biblical verses and argues that they point toward an allegorical meaning typically in line with Hellenistic virtues. Some rabbis, though more restrained than Philo, also employ what we might call an allegorical method of linking biblical verses and scenes to other, seemingly unrelated events. Yet for both there is no denial of the real referents of the

Bible (in contrast to Origen's method; see below).[23] Both insist on the abiding authority of the biblical text even when "loosening" verses from their literal referents. Philo famously rebukes those who, carried away by allegory, neglect the actual demands of the Law.[24] The effect of allegorization is not to undermine the binding authority of the text, especially its legal requirements, but to uncover additional, even unexpected meanings in it.

Origen extensively relies on allegorical interpretation, which serves numerous important goals (Hom. on Gen 6:1). At least in theory, his hermeneutical rule is clear: "with respect to Holy Scripture, our opinion is that the whole of it has a 'spiritual' [i.e., allegorical], but not the whole a 'bodily' meaning, because the bodily meaning is in many places impossible." In practice, Origen adopts a freewheeling approach to the Bible, often entirely rejecting as "bodily" any straightforward interpretation of a verse in its context in order to discover what he calls "hidden treasures of wisdom and knowledge" (First Principles 4:19-23). Origen could quickly move far from the biblical text, not just introducing topics that he thought were relevant but seemingly jettisoning the biblical text itself. The allegorical meaning is typically a Christological reading, persuasive to believers but obviously completely untenable to Jews.[25]

Besides passages objectionable for their anthropomorphic or unflattering portraits of God, passages that present impractical or impossible demands are likewise allegorized so as to not be mandatory. Seemingly onerous restrictions on travel during the Sabbath; bans on eating certain animals that are hard to identify; even the parapet that one is required by biblical law to build on a roof: all are allegorized out of existence and given spiritual meanings.[26] This allows him to claim the Hebrew Bible as his community's religious text, while freeing him up both to reject all that is unacceptable in it (e.g., many ritual commandments) and to posit connections between ancient passages and Jesus. Though he relies on a distinctive allegorical method, the result is familiar to us from Paul and Irenaeus. This is because Origen saw himself above all as an exegete for the Christian community, in service of the Church. In his case as well, the authority of the Bible to compel certain forms of behavior could be compromised by the practical needs of his Gentile community to retain the Bible while also rejecting much of it.

Discussion

The topic of biblical authority provoked intensive discussions and debates among early Christian writers. All of those surveyed here face the same fundamental challenge: how to affirm biblical authority in some ways while rejecting it in others. They deny the binding authority of most if not all the legal commandments of the Hebrew Bible. These conclusions, however broadly shared among Christians, directly clash with most Jews' understandings of biblical authority. This inevitably divides the two communities, for out of a shared text emerge mutually exclusive claims.[27]

In the context of modern Jewish-Christian relations, we face here a distinctively Christian scandal of particularity. The underlying social reality of early Christianity—the emergence of majority- or exclusively Gentile churches—encouraged these particular readings of the Bible that legitimated this development, and which is largely normative through the present. These writers, unlike the gnostics, come from communities that refuse to reject the Bible but likewise refuse to impose its many onerous requirements on their members. At the time, practical or missionary concerns, among others, stood in the way of commandments such as circumcision and food laws in their communities. By contrast, non-Christian Jews, and some Jewish Christians, were uninterested in forming such religious communities, and therefore did not reject biblical authority as unacceptably coercive. Without this particular context, Jews inevitably found and find such Christian biblical readings scandalous.

Likewise scandalous to Jews is the writers' explicitly Christological hermeneutic, in which they largely see the Hebrew Bible from this particular perspective. This should not be construed too narrowly; not every verse is read as a prophetic foreshadowing of Jesus. Nonetheless, the Bible's authority is largely understood as a guide to Christian religious life, which includes its role as a reliable witness to and resource for understanding Jesus, and also includes a broader role in shaping the rituals, behaviors, and organization of Christian communities.[28] This hermeneutic naturally shapes all views of the authority and the influence of the text, because certain parts of the text, and certain roles for the text, are privileged over others. Sections of laws, for example, are downplayed, in favor of sections on eschatology or the fate of the Gentiles. In all cases, decisions about authority should be seen as negotiations about the Bible's relevance. The text's influence is naturally greatest in those areas of religious life where the community places the greatest emphasis. For the formative early Christian generations, the emphasis was on the humanity and person of Jesus and the creation of a new religious movement separate from the Jews and Judaism.[29]

In my focus on biblical authority, and the specific claims made for the text by early Christians, I hope to have provided both modern Jews and Christians a clearer understanding of the *reasons* for these conclusions, and the *reasoning* used by those who formulated them. This fuller understanding is vital, because in modern inter-religious dialogue and Jewish-Christian relations, the conclusions that are reached by individual writers are not the only things that are relevant. Theological assumptions need to be made explicit, and the reasoning process needs to be visible, for only then is a sympathetic if critical discussion possible.

Also, context is key, for Christian views of biblical authority arose in the highly unsettled early period and yet they determined (perhaps circumscribed) all subsequent thought. For example, Paul's need to rebut Jewish Christian counter-missionaries in the mid-first century differs from Irenaeus' and Origen's anti-gnostic polemic. With this fuller knowledge, Christians can better relate to their own traditions by recognizing how these conclusions were reached, and what factors were influential. It is surely not my hope (or even my place to hope) that modern Christians' understanding of the reasons and reasoning behind these views of biblical authority will prompt doubts or questions about them. Rather, it is to move discussion beyond the simplistic sense of an unbridgeable, even primordial opposition between Jews and Christians regarding the Bible, and to see the contingency and complexity of the arguments used to support the claims.

For Jews, the goal is similar, and in my discussion I seek to overcome widespread ignorance about this subject. Christian thought on the topic of biblical authority is complex, and it is tempting to assume that all Christians, because of agreement on some issues, use the same logic for the same reasons. The largely over-simplistic judgment many Jews hold—Christians just neglect or entirely dispense with the Hebrew Bible—is a result both of indifference and of centuries of religious polemics, which encourages participants to highlight the most extreme positions and also those most unfavorable to one's opponents. In the latter case, accusations of inconsistency by Jewish anti-Christian polemicists focused on the tensions in Christian views.[30] Furthermore, disagreements reflect different ideas about the nature of biblical authority, which Jews traditionally analyze in terms of binding requirements for ritual and moral actions.[31]

My stated goal of providing a clearer understanding of deep differences may appear inauspicious for future dialogue. However, the reasons and reasoning of these early Christians in their discussions of biblical authority, regardless of the conclusions they reach, can certainly be conducive to dialogue, for these take us beyond the simple claim that Jews and Christians fundamentally disagree about how to read the Bible. The challenges of making an ancient text relevant, of adapting to new circumstances, are relevant to Jews and Christians alike; Jews, in their own contexts, do much the same. Even the methods used by these Christian interpreters are deeply indebted to Jewish midrash and exegesis. Out of a sympathetic and learned engagement with the traditions and beliefs of another tradition, something that has only begun to happen, Jews and Christians will hopefully deepen their discussions of this complex topic.

Notes

1. Muslims of course also revere the Bible, or more specifically some of the biblical narratives, as an earlier form of divine communication. However, the actual text plays a far less prominent role. Also, there are many differences between Jewish and Christian versions of the Hebrew Bible, such as the name itself (the Jews' Tanakh or the Christians' Old Testament) and the order of the books.
2. von Campenhausen, Hans, *The Formation of the Christian Bible*, trans. J. A. Baker (Mifflintown, PA: Sigler, 1997), 1–102.
3. See the introduction in Brown, William P., ed., *Engaging Biblical Authority: Perspectives on the Bible as Scripture* (Louisville: Westminster John Knox, 2007), ix–xvi.
4. See von Campenhausen, *Formation*, 1-102; Heine, Ronald E., *Reading the Old Testament with the Ancient Church: Exploring the Formation of Early Christian Thought* (Grand Rapid, MI: Baker, 2007), 47–74.
5. I do not consider the presentation of Jesus' views of the Law in the Gospels. Not only do these vary between the Gospels, complicating attempts at synthesis, but they are of limited relevance, especially when most traditionally Jewish in affirming the continuing obligation to observe the Law (e.g. in Matthew). In an increasingly Gentile church, they are largely ignored or rejected. On the marginalization of Law-observance (i.e. so-called Jewish Christianity), see Dunn, James D. G., *Unity and Diversity in the New Testament: An Inquiry into*

the Character of Earliest Christianity, second edition (Valley Forge, PA: Trinity Press International, 1990), 235–66.

6. See the essays in Porter, Stanley, ed. *Paul and his Opponents* (Leiden: Brill, 2005). Scholars now generally refrain from presuming that the opponents in the different churches are all related or represent one single faction.

7. Greer, Rowan A., "The Christian Bible and Its Interpretation," in *Early Biblical Interpretation*, ed. James L. Kugel and Rowan A. Greer (Philadelphia: Westminster, 1986), 113–14. This position faces its first serious threat in the second century from gnostic and Marcionite Christians, who reject the Hebrew Bible; see below. On the much-disputed term gnosticism, see King, Karen L., *What is Gnosticism?* (Cambridge: Belknap, 2003).

8. In general, his demands for "life in the Spirit"—rejection of idolatry, sexual misdeeds, etc.—reflect biblical teachings (Gal 5:13–26). See Sanders, E. P. *Paul, the Law, and the Jewish People* (Minneapolis: Fortress, 1983), 99.

9. Greer, "The Christian Bible," 126, 134; von Campenhausen, *Formation*, 32.

10. This is arguably the most contested topic in Pauline thought; a helpful recent collection of essays on this topic is Dunn, James D. G., ed., *Paul and the Mosaic Law* (Grand Rapids, MI: Eerdmans, 2001).

11. A seminal work on Paul in his missionary context is Stendahl, Krister, "The Apostle Paul and the Introspective Conscience of the West," in *Paul Among Jews and Gentiles* (Philadelphia: Fortress, 1976), 78–96.

12. This is debatable; Rom 3:23-24 suggests this; also, Luke provides some evidence of this accusation, in Acts 21:20–21.

13. See Gaston, Lloyd, *Paul and the Torah* (Vancouver: University of British Columbia Press, 1987).

14. See also Greer, "The Christian Bible," 155–76; von Campenhausen, *Formation*, 142–268.

15. He charges the Jews with being less observant than Christians, for they add to and subtract from the Law, and do not act with altruistic motives (4:12:4).

16. There are some parallels to this emphasis on the Decalogue in Paul's writings as well (e.g., Rom 13:8–10), though unlike Irenaeus he is not explicit about this.

17. On changing views of the Sabbath and the move to Sunday worship, see Bradshaw, Paul F., *The Search for the Origins of Christian Worship: Sources and Methods for the Study of Early Liturgy*, Second edition (Oxford: Oxford University Press: 2002), 178–82.

18. See also Chester, Andrew, "Messianism, Torah, and Early Christian Tradition," in *Tolerance and Intolerance in Early Judaism and Christianity*, ed. Graham N. Stanton and Guy G. Stroumsa (Cambridge: Cambridge University Press, 1998), 330–32.

19. Cited in the Philocalia, a later collection of his writings, at 1:28; see von Campenhausen, *Formation*, 308.

20. See Blowers, Paul M., "Origen, the Rabbis, and the Bible: Toward a Picture of Judaism and Christianity in Third-Century Caesarea," in *Origen of Alexandria: His World and His Legacy*, ed. Charles Kannengiesser and William L. Petersen (Notre Dame: University of Notre Dame Press, 1988), 111-13; R. P. C. Hanson, *Allegory and Event: A Study of the Sources and Significance of Origen's Interpretation of Scripture* (Louisville: Westminster John Knox, 2003), 362, 368.

21. Bammel, C. P., "Law and Temple in Origen," in *Temple Amicitiae: Essays on the Second Temple Presented to Ernst Bammel*, ed. William Horbury (Sheffield: Sheffield Academic Press, 1991).

22. In his views on allegorical interpretation, he was also influenced by Paul (e.g., Gal 4:24) and non-Jewish Hellenistic writers; see Joseph W. Trigg, *Origen* (London and New York: Routledge, 1998), 12–13.
23. See the discussion and references in Hanson, *Allegory*, 11–36.
24. The Migration of Abraham 89–93.
25. Clark, Elizabeth A., *Reading Renunciation: Asceticism and Scripture in Early Christianity* (Princeton, NJ: Princeton University Press, 1999), 68; Hanson, *Allegory*, 371.
26. E.g., Comm. on Matt 17:7; Comm. on Romans 2:9; Celsus 2:2; 5:48; First Principles 4:17; see Hanson, *Allegory*, 307–08.
27. This is not to suggest that, unlike Christians, Jews were or are literal interpreters of Scripture; their readings can be allegorical, and sometimes fanciful and far-fetched.
28. As scholars now recognize, there was in fact no clean, early break between Judaism and Christianity, or between Jews and Christians. The desire to demarcate sharp boundaries for religious communities was largely a goal of elite religious leaders, Jewish and especially Christian, and undermined in reality in many places and times; see Becker, Adam and Reed, Annette Yoshiko, eds., *The Ways that Never Parted: Jews & Christians in Late Antiquity & the Early Middle Ages* (Tübingen: Mohr Siebeck, 2003).
29. See the introduction in Brown, ed., *Biblical Authority*, xiii.
30. Interestingly, such criticisms appear in Christian texts; from the first few centuries, see Justin's Dialogue with Trypho 10 and Origen's Celsus 2:1–6.
31. To give one example: Marc Brettler, when analyzing tensions in Jewish understandings of authority, revealingly chooses as his examples detailed festival laws and food laws, in Brettler, Marc Zvi, "Biblical Authority: A Jewish Pluralistic View," in *Engaging Biblical Authority: Perspectives on the Bible as Scripture*, ed. William P. Brown (Louisville: Westminster John Knox), 5.

TRAVELING IN DIFFERENT DIRECTIONS ON THE LITURGICAL HIGHWAY

Karen Marie Yust

In her children's book, *In God's Name*, Rabbi Sandy Eisenberg Sasso chronicles a people's attempts to describe God. She suggests that the context and life experiences of individuals shape what they call God. "The tired soldier who fought too many wars called God *Maker of Peace*" (Sasso 1994:10), she writes, and "[t]he artist who carved figures from the earth's hard stone called God *My Rock*" (Sasso 1994:11). "The young woman who nursed her newborn son called God *Mother*" (Sasso 1994:20), she continues, "[a]nd the child who was lonely called God *Friend*" (Sasso 1994:23). Sasso's storybook characters highlight the interplay between theological concepts and mundane life. The language that a congregation, whether Jewish or Christian, uses to worship God is inextricably bound up in the activities and experiences of that congregation in the ordinary passage of days.

Lawrence Hoffman, in reflecting on the development of Jewish worship resources, observes, "Prayerbooks, then, whatever else they may be theologically, are also social documents. New prayerbooks represent a new social context" (Hoffman 1977:134). He recognizes that worship language evolves according to the shifting experiences of those who evoke that language. The linguistic, visual and kinesthetic aspects of this language are all shaped by human engagement in the world, so that even the choreography of a prayer service and the aesthetics of the space in which it occurs reflect the self-perception of the participating worshippers (Hoffman 1977:159). When this correspondence between worship language and life experience fragments, people of faith agitate for new worship resources that better reflect their daily existence. As Hoffman notes with regard to orders of worship developed during the Creative Liturgy movement of the mid-twentieth century, "these services provide their own message in which content (manifest and symbolic), structure, and choreography all combine to give a consistent picture of American Judaism as defined by the services' authors" (Hoffman 1977:151).

Alexander Schmemann offers a similar observation about Christian worship. Reflecting on Orthodox Christian practices, Schmemann suggests that, for many congregations, "the deciding factors are taste, local tradition and custom" (Schmemann 1996:37) in determining the shape and language of worship. Comparing common worship with the Ordo (rubrics established by tradition as liturgical norms), he concludes that contemporary worshippers are often indifferent to traditional structures for worship. He writes, "The Ordo is not denied in principle. But it remains simply as a kind of background, allowing the most 'popular' moments of worship to stand out and be performed with maximum effect" (Schmemann 1996:38). Schmemann's concern is that worship practices are becoming "ends in themselves" (Schmemann 1996:38) rather than components of a larger whole that link a congregation with a transcendent God.

And yet, as both Jewish and Christian liturgical scholars know, a community's worship does not simply portray its current cultural identity. Hoffman explains that "the prayerbook message...does more than merely reflect an already existent community image[;]...we must extend our understanding of the message to allow for its capacity to change the community's identity" (Hoffman 1977:146). This change in part occurs because the content of a prayer service offers "a variety of statements of faith with which the worshippers are asked to identify" (Hoffman 1977:141). Gordon Lathrop suggests that Christian worship involves "juxtaposing an old book [the scriptures] and this present people" (Lathrop 1998:16), which has required Christians to negotiate the meaning and embodiment of faith throughout history. Such negotiation makes room for dissonant meanings and alternative experiences of God's presence within Christian liturgy.

Thus, some of the faith statements and negotiated meanings contained within liturgies challenge the assumptions and experiences of participants, which can lead to questions. Sasso points to this situation in her children's story: "Sometimes the people who called God by different names were puzzled. They said, 'Every living thing has a single name: the marigold, pansy and lily; the oak tree, sequoia and pine'. God must have a single name that is greater and more wonderful than all other names" (Sasso 1994:13). Human beings may feel compelled to contain liturgical language within narrow definitions of what constitutes proper worship, but this impulse is simultaneously challenged by the polyphony of experiences and traditional expressions brought together in the work of the worshipping community. As Lathrop observes, "For Christians, all texts and all rituals are the wrong words. All have to be broken to speak the Christian faith..." (Lathrop 1998:50). He wants to emphasize the limitations of human language in speaking about God and God's activity in the world, yet his assertion also underscores the need for a dynamic understanding of liturgy. Hoffman frames this dynamism somewhat differently. He reminds us that Jews may eschew traditional liturgical language in part because they seek "a new perspective on themselves" that can only come through experimentation with new ways of praying together (Hoffman 1977:151). Thus, while prayerbooks are "the community's major contact with primary Jewish sources" (Hoffman 1977:132), the development of new prayerbooks has been "synonymous with the evolution of the Jewish community" (Hoffman 1977:133). Jewish worshippers negotiate new meaning in the interstices of traditional texts and shifting contextual experiences. This is also true for Christians, although the language of liturgical discourse in some Christian circles tends more toward questions of whether worship positions participants within the traditionally Jewish identities of "the People of God, a royal priesthood, a chosen people, the Body of Christ" (Schmemann 1996:38) than toward explorations of how social context distinctively shapes Christian identity today.

One might explain these different emphases—the brokenness of human language about the divine and the predictable reconstruction of communal identity in relation to context—in terms of different normative assumptions about worship practices. Lathrop constructs his argument in terms of an eschatological conception of God's just realm as the primary measure by which worship is assessed. He writes, "The dominion of God is to be an order and pattern of things that is far greater than—and therefore deeply critical of—ritual order of any kind. Ritual order always has its outsiders: its women, its leaven, its sinners. The dominion of God has no outsiders" (Lathrop 1998:26). One might argue that Jewish scholars begin not with the universal character of God's dominion as liturgical norm, but with the peculiar and significant status of "insider/outsider" accorded the Jewish people theologically and socially. The Jewish people are those whom God has chosen as the people of God *and* those whom other nations have demonized and sought to exterminate. The Christian adoption of Jewish religious identity can be interpreted as a supercessionist attempt to redefine the beliefs that make one a genuine theological insider, even if Christian scholars prefer to characterize this adoption as an enlargement of God's family. Insisting that God's dominion is without membership boundaries circumscribes the role of "personal historical consciousness" (Langer 2005:13) in liturgical formation and practice. How, then, can Christians appreciate a traditional Jewish liturgy that "portrays its community, Israel, as distinctive among human communities" (Langer 2005:12)? Even modern Jewish liturgies, which Ruth Langer says "reflect a tension between the desire to maintain a particularistic sense of Jewish identity and the need theologically to justify the modern community's participation in the larger world" (Langer 2005:18), bump up against such a Christian norm of a divinely ordained open society.

Perhaps, this is why the presenters for our colloquium discussion about "Worship and the Particularity of the Other" structured their remarks in such vastly different ways.[1] Lawrence Hoffman drew attention to the many forms of difference—interreligious, interdenominational, intra-denominational, and intra-congregational—that have shaped and continue to inform Jewish liturgical practices. Martha Moore-Keish focused on Christian faithfulness to the Ordo and its function as a framework upon which cultures build liturgies. The former invited us to struggle with the messiness of differences, the latter to rest in the assurance of an underlying sameness. Both desire that liturgy function as a guide to understanding human identity and humanity's relationship with the divine. But the decision to begin conversation immersed in contextual differences rather than build a conversation on a fundamental framework leads to quite different ways of assessing the theological and practical norms of worship. Hoffman's approach evaluates the appropriateness of Jewish worship in terms of how well it conforms to a moral concept of Jewish peoplehood contextualized by its expression within contemporary Jewish cultures. Moore-Keish contends that Christian worship is most faithful when it conforms to the endoskeletal structure of the Ordo and is then enfleshed in ways appropriate to particular cultures. "Peoplehood" and "Ordo" are distinctive normative plumb lines that underscore the particularity, the "otherness" of Jewish and Christian worship and complicate interreligious dialogue between these cousins in faith.

However, Sasso's storybook encourages us to imagine the God who is the focus of worship as a deity who revels in both particularity and oneness. She writes, "Then each person... called out their names for God ... all at the same time. At that moment the people knew that all the names for God were good, and no name was better than another. Then all at once their voices came together and they called God *One*" (Sasso 1994:29–31). While Sasso begins, as the other Jewish thinkers in this article have done, with difference, she pronounces God's benediction on the drawing together of differences into oneness. Is it not possible, then, that Christian thinkers might work this process from the other direction, beginning with oneness and receiving God's blessing on the refracting of that oneness into different expressions of divine identity? As conversations about worship continue between Jews and Christians, we would do well to recognize that we may be moving in different directions but we share the same liturgical highway. In the rest stops stationed along the road, we can compare notes regarding where we have been and what we have learned about God and ourselves thus far. We can advise one another about bumpy patches in the road in need of theological repaving so that our liturgical practices maintain integrity. We can challenge one another to continually reexamine our preferences for distinctiveness or underlying sameness so that we do not fall in liturgical sinkholes, such as worship structures too closely tied only to ethnic traditions (Hoffman) or that use the Ordo as a privacy fence to screen out all change rather than as a framework that welcomes appropriate cultural expressions of faith (Moore-Keish). Jews may be heading to Jerusalem and Christians into all the world, but talking together about why and how we worship enables all of us to examine our liturgical assumptions and shape more faithful liturgical forms. In this, our particularity contributes to a shared goal: worship that helps us remember who and whose we are.

Works cited

Hoffman, Lawrence, 1977, "The Liturgical Message," in Lawrence Hoffman, ed., *Gates of Understanding*, New York: Central Conference of American Rabbis, pp. 131–68.

Langer, Ruth, 2005, "Theologies of Self and Other in American Jewish Liturgies," *CCAR Journal: A Reform Jewish Quarterly*, Winter 2005, pp. 3–41.

Lathrop, Gordon, 1998, *Holy Things: A Liturgical Theology*, Minneapolis: Fortress Press.

Sasso, Sandy Eisenberg, 1994, *In God's Name*, Woodstock, VT: Jewish Lights Publishing.

Schmemann, Alexander, 1996, *Introduction to Liturgical Theology*, Crestwood, NY: St. Vladimir's Seminary Press.

Note

1. References to Hoffman's and Moore-Keish's ideas in the latter half of this article come from my notes re: presentations at the fifth meeting of "The Scandal of Particularity" colloquium, held in Richmond, VA, March 2–4, 2008.

LAND AS AN ISSUE IN CHRISTIAN-JEWISH DIALOGUE

John T. Pawlikowski

Two tendencies played a prominent role in shaping the Christian outlook on the issue of the Jewish People and the land of Israel over the centuries. These tendencies have their roots in the early centuries of Christianity. The first of these tendencies was the so-called theology of "perpetual wandering" perspective with respect to the Jewish People. This theology became so imbedded in popular Western culture that even a plant came to bear its name.

According to the "perpetual wandering" theology, Christians look upon Jews as forever relegated to the status of "displaced persons" among the nations of the world. A prevailing mindset is evident in many of the patristic writings. When the "veil of the Temple was rent" and the covenant between God and his people broken permanently as a result, Jews received "a bill of divorce," as it where, and from that time onwards they were doomed to roam restless over the face of the earth.

This perpetual wandering theology continued in force throughout Christian history into the modern period. The noted biblical scholar who in fact defended Nazism Gerhard Kittel and served as editor of the very influential *Theological Dictionary of the New Testament*[1] viewed post-biblical Judaism as largely a community in dispersion. "Authentic Judaism," he wrote "abides by the symbol of the stranger wandering restless and homeless on the face of the earth." And even the great Cardinal Augustin Bea, who played such a central role in the development, passage and initial implementation of Vatican II's historic *Nostra Aetate,* revealed continued traces of a traditional Catholic mindset regarding Jews, the covenant and the land. In a 1966 work titled *The Church and the Jewish People.* Bea falls into the use of language quite reminiscent of perpetual wandering theology. "The fate of Jerusalem," he tells us, "constitutes a sort of final reckoning at the end of a thousand years of infidelities and opposition to God." From that point onward, Bea insists, Jews and Judaism existed merely as a "witness to their iniquity and to the truth of the Christian faith."[2] It is understandable, therefore, according to Bea, why many Christian bodies reacted to the reestablishment of the modern State of Israel in 1948 with considerable consternation and even outright opposition. And we also need to recall that in 1904 when Pope Pius X received Theodore Herzl, the founder of the modern Zionist effort to restore a Jewish state in occupied Palestine, the Pope ultimately offered a theological explanation for his unwillingness to support this effort. In his perspective since Jews did not accept Jesus Christ he could never endorse the notion of a Jewish national homeland—clearly shades of a perpetual wandering theology—even though he indicated to Herzl that he was in no position to stop this effort.[3]

From the above brief sample of Christian approaches to the question of Jews and the land beginning in the Patristic era, it should be evident that a long tradition exists within Christianity of an explicitly theological approach to the land of Israel. In fact, it is fair to say that rarely, if ever, in Christian history has Israel been merely regarded as a "political" issue for the churches. Any adequate understanding of Judaism's attachment to the land within a Christian context must begin with a clear acknowledgment that the churches basically rejected this attachment for explicitly Christian theological reasons.

While chapter four of *Nostra Aetate* is a very brief statement in comparison to most other documents from Vatican II, it in fact contains the seeds of a major theological revolution that undercut the validity of the classical "perpetual wandering" theology of Judaism within the churches. For, in asserting that there never existed any basis for a blanket accusation of deicide and in affirming the continuing validity of Jewish covenantal participation after the Christ Event and the bondedness that Christians and Jews now share through the covenant, *Nostra Aetate* decisively undercut the foundation of the displacement/perpetual wandering theology of the Jewish People that had dominated Christian theological and popular thinking for two millennia.

For that reason it is quite accurate to argue that the full political recognition of the State of Israel by the Holy See in December 1993 represents the ultimate recognition of that repudiation by Vatican II. The coffin on displacement/perpetual wandering theology had been finally sealed. The formal recognition of Israel helps to create for the first time a situation of a partnership rooted in fundamental equality by eliminating a major component of the traditional theology of covenantal displacement and perpetual homeless for the Jews.

The second major theological tendency within Christianity over the centuries with regard to post-Easter Jewish claims to the land has been focused on efforts by Christian theologians to replace a supposedly exclusive Jewish emphasis on "earthly" Israel with a stress on a "heavenly" Jerusalem and an eschatological Zion. Emergence of the term "holy land" as the basic referent for this region has been part and parcel of this overall theological tendency. While this tendency certainly has not exercised the same disastrous impact on Christian attitudes toward the Jewish people and their rights to the land, it nonetheless, however more subtly, had the effect of neutralizing (if not actually undercutting) continued Jewish claims. The bottom line of this theological approach was without question that the authentic claims to the land had now passed over into the hands of the Christians. "Jerusalem," spiritually and territorially, now belonged to the Christians. Neither Muslims nor Jews could control the city after the coming of Christ and it became a holy duty for the Crusaders to return it to Christian hands no matter what the amount of bloodshed involved. The origins of this Christian perspective are to be seen in parts of the New Testament itself. The Letter to the Hebrews and the Book of Revelation are two key books in terms of the development of this viewpoint.

But once again, as with the covenantal displacement/perpetual wandering theology, the real growth of this theological outlook on the land took place during the Patristic era. It began with Justin Martyr in the second century. In his famous *Dialogue with Trypho*, the first major post-biblical work on Christian-Jewish relations, Justin took up the question of the possible rebuilding of the destroyed city of Jerusalem and what significance this might hold for the Christian community. He expressed his belief that indeed such a rebuilding will take place. "I and others who are 'right-thinking' Christians on all points are convinced that there will be a resurrection of the dead and a thousand-year (period) in which Jerusalem will be (re)built, adorned and enlarged, as the prophets Ezekiel and Isaiah and others declare."[4]

In another part of *the Dialogue with Trypho*, Justin introduced for the first time the term "holy land" into the Christian vocabulary. In this section, he contrasted the possession of the land under Joshua with the possession to come upon the return of Christ. In the former case, the possession was only temporary; in the latter case it will be eternal.

For Justin, the approach to the land promises, though eschatological, was concrete and territorial. But the real descendants of Abraham were now the Christians not the Jews (something that Trypho naturally cannot accept). While Christians may not yet have the land, one day they will. The transfer of ownership has in fact taken place. It was this theological vision which eventually would serve as the backbone of the Crusaders' drive for the restoration of Jerusalem and the Holy Land to Christian hands that resulted in the loss of countless Muslim and Jewish lives. The term, "Holy Land," thus surfaced in the Christian vocabulary in the context of eschatology and as a direct replacement for Jewish longings for Zion. As Robert Wilken has put it in *The Land Called Holy*:

> Within Jewish tradition eschatology and restoration were almost synonymous, and for Justin eschatology meant a future rebuilding of Jerusalem at the return of Christ. Christian hopes for the future were rooted in the land promise to Abraham and in the words of the prophets about the glorification of Jerusalem. To be sure, the hope of restoration was modified in light of the Resurrection of Jesus; there would be no temple in the restored Jerusalem. Yet Christian eschatologyremained wedded to the earth, retaining the realistic features of the restorationist tradition. As Irenaeus would insist, the new Jerusalem would be located "under heaven."[5]

While this "Holy Land" approach to Palestine does not directly attack the Jewish community in the same way as the "perpetual wandering" theology, it nonetheless has a similar result in the end. Jews no longer retain any claim to the land of Palestine. The concrete historical views of Justin and Irenaeus would eventually, however, give way to a far more "heavenly" interpretation of the Holy Land and especially of its center, Jerusalem. This perspective emerged in the writings of Origen and was confirmed by his disciple, Eusebius.

Though some within the Christian community continued to cling rather tenaciously to a vision of a restored Jerusalem in the Holy Land, they were forced to give way in the end to the arguments of Origen who, in the third century, interpreted the spiritual prophecies about Jerusalem and the land in general in an entirely spiritual way. His stated goal was to dispel the mistaken view held by Christians that the land promised by God to the righteous pertains at all to the land of Judea. In the perspective of Origen, the Pauline texts that speak of Jerusalem do not in fact describe an earthly city but rather one existing in the heavens. This "heavenly Jerusalem" is destined ultimately to replace the earthly Jerusalem. It was Origen's contention that this understanding in fact constituted the authentic interpretation of the prophetic texts as well. Jews had erred in applying them to an earthly realm. Again, this "heavenly Jerusalem" theology, while not as overtly anti-Jewish as the "perpetual wandering" theology had in fact the same bottom line: Jews had no valid religious claims to the land.

With the formal establishment of the modern State of Israel by the United Nations in 1948 these "anti-land" theologies relative to the Jewish People in classical Christian thought came under intense pressure, especially in Catholicism where the Holy See had to react to this establishment. In light of Pope Pius X's response to Theodore Herzl in 1904 cited earlier tremendous hesitation developed within Vatican circles about political recognition of the new state. The initial decision was to deny formal recognition though in all candor evidence has now surfaced in Israeli archives that many of the country's leaders were not actually eager for such recognition lest it enhance the Catholic Church's claims regarding Jerusalem.[6] When Pope Paul VI visited the Holy Land during his papacy he allowed almost no political recognition of his presence in the country and never referred to the State in any public address.

Gradually, however, the Holy See's position was modified to the point where by the early 1970s "de facto" recognition was accorded Israel in the sense that Israeli and Vatican diplomatic officials now held official exchanges even though full, formal diplomatic recognition continued to be withheld. In the initial discussion regarding the proposed text of the 1974 Vatican Guidelines on Catholic-Jewish Relations issued to commemorate the tenth anniversary of chapter four of *Nostra Aetate* a section on the State of Israel was to be included in light of *Nostra Aetate's* undercutting of the "perpetual wandering" theology as a result of its insistence on continued Jewish covenantal inclusion. But a premature release of this information led to its removal from the final version of the statement. But the impetus for full or "de jure" recognition did not grind to a complete halt. In fact the Guidelines most-quoted line about the need for Christians to come to understand Jews "as they define themselves" strengthened the necessity for the Church to recognize the deep-seated attachment to the land as a hallmark of authentic Jewish self-identity.

Two other documents further enhanced the movement toward formal recognition of Israel. The first occurred in a 1984 document *Redemptionis Anno* from the pen of Pope John Paul II. In this document he anticipated the formal recognition that came to fruition later on in his papacy: "For the Jewish People who live in the State of Israel and who preserve in that land such precious testimonies of their history and their faith, we must ask for the desired security and the due tranquility that is the prerogative of every nation and condition of life and of progress of every society."[7] This statement clearly exhibits on the part of John Paul II a sense of the deep intertwining of faith and land within the Jewish People.

The 1985 *Notes on the Correct Way to Present the Jews and Judaism in Preaching and Catechesis in the Roman Catholic Church* which commemorated the twentieth anniversary of *Nostra Aetate,* added to the process of Christian reflection on the meaning of land in terms of Judaism within Catholicism, especially when we contrast what is said in this document with the classical Christian outlook rooted in the theologies of "perpetual wandering" and the "heavenly Jerusalem." Two statements in the documents are especially relevant for this discussion. The first affirms that "The history of Israel did not end in seventy A.D. . . . It continued, especially in a numerous Diaspora which allowed Israel to carry to the whole world a witness . . . while preserving the memory of the land of their forefathers at the heart of their hope." The second argues that "The permanence of Israel (while so many ancient peoples have disappeared without a trace) is a historic fact and a sign to be interpreted within God's design."[8] Clearly, these statements repudiate the classical "displacement theology."

This gradual process of removing theological objections within Catholicism to the idea of an independent Jewish state, as has already been noted, reached its climax in the December 30, 1993 signing of the Fundamental Agreement between the Holy See and the State of Israel. While primarily a political agreement, it clearly has been read by major Catholic and Jewish leaders such as Rabbi David Rosen, the late Cardinal John O'Connor as well as Cardinal William Keeler and the then U.S. Ambassador to the Vatican Raymond Flynn as bringing to an end the difficult history in Christian-Jewish relations regarding Jewish territorial dreams. While it remains legitimate for Catholic leaders to criticize this or that particular policy of an Israeli government all basis for arguing theologically against the idea of a Jewish national state has been permanently eradicated. The document itself links the Fundamental Agreement to the overall effort begun at the II Vatican Council to set the Christian-Jewish relationship on a path of reconciliation, growth in mutual understanding, and friendship.

In other Christian communities that do not involve themselves in the formal recognition of nation-states as does the Holy See, the process of removing remaining vestiges of the "perpetual wandering" theology of Judaism has been somewhat less dramatic but nonetheless quite real. Any number of Christian communities have publicly acknowledged the Jewish ties to the land of Israel as an authentic dimension of the Jewish religious perspective over the past several decades. But we have also witnessed a strong critique in certain sectors of Protestant Christianity that has called for divestment from Israel and strongly rebuked notions of Christian Zionism. While there is no question that significant sectors of the Christian Zionist community have gone beyond legitimate theological boundaries in bestowing an internal Christian theological meaning on the State of Israel while failing to offer any critique whatsoever of its specific policies towards Palestinians, the attack on Christian Zionism has often seemed to deny any legitimacy to Jewish theological interpretations of the State. While echoes of a similar critique have surfaced in some parts of the Catholic social justice community, the voices have generally not been as loud and intense and have not been endorsed at the level of the Vatican.

In addition to official Christian documents, individual theologians, both Protestant and Catholic, have reflected on the significance of the reestablishment of the State of Israel. While no clear consensus has emerged, perspectives have been offered that contain the seeds of further development.

Leading Catholic theologian David Tracy, in discussions relative to the theological significance of the Holocaust, saw the issue of a Jewish theology of the land within a broader setting of a return to the significance of history within the Christian community. Tracy has long been an advocate of such a return. So, while he offered no specific understanding of the Jewish land tradition from a Christian theological perspective, he clearly acknowledged the legitimacy of such a discussion if one grounds theological discussion within the context of history. By implication Tracy was suggesting that the problem that many Christians past and present have had with theological discussions regarding Israel is rooted in an inadequate historical basis for theology where the tendency has been strong to see theology as exclusively supernatural and standing apart from an historical context. The patristic discussion regarding Jerusalem, discussed above, might be seen as one example of the tendency Tracy is rightly critiquing. Other Catholic scholars such as John Oesterreicher, Charlotte Klein. Bruce Williams and Kurt Hruby have also taken up consideration of the place of Israel in Christian theology. Williams and Klein have been particularly strong in emphasizing a specifically redemptive dimension to the State of Israel from the Christian perspective, though in a manner quite different from that of many Christian Zionists where the notion of Israel tends to lose specific Jewish meaning. On the Protestant side J. Coos Schoneveld, Walter Harrelson, and Alan Davies are scholars who have expressed similar views. An excellent summary of Catholic positions in the initial stages of this discussion can be found in the late Anthony Kenny's volume *Catholics, Jews and the State of Israel.*[9]

No consensus currently exists among the relatively few Christian theologians who have taken up the land question. In my own personal reflections on the place of the land in Christian thought, three issues remain central. They are not easily integrated. First, I would certainly wish to maintain some significant differences between Christianity and Judaism regarding the present meaning of the biblical land tradition. It is my firm belief that one result of the Christian theology of the Incarnation is an equalization of all land in terms of sacredness. While Jerusalem and the Holy Land may evoke a certain spiritual and historical significance for Christians from the standpoint of theological principle they are no more sacred than Geneva, Rome, Rio, or Chicago. Second, I do clearly acknowledge the centrality of the land to the basic definition of covenant within Judaism.

Professor Ruth Langer rightly challenged me on this point in her response to my plenary presentation at the international conference at the Pontifical Gregorian University in Rome in September 2005. She also makes the point about the centrality of land for Jewish religious identity in an essay published in the electronic journal of the Council of Centers on Jewish-Christian Relations.[10] If we take seriously the central assertion in the 1974 Vatican Guidelines about the need for Christians to come to understand Jews as they define themselves, then there is simply no way of ignoring the land question which, as Langer clearly demonstrates in her recent article, is a central component of contemporary identity both for religious and secular Jews. And third, since I affirm from a theological perspective an inherent bonding between the Church and the Jewish People, I recognize that the Jewish sense of land as integral to the understanding of covenant makes some claims on my faith as well. This is especially the case if we understand the Jewish and Christian covenants as distinctive, but integrated, as Cardinal Walter Kasper, President of the Holy See's Commission for Religious Relations with the Jews, has strongly argued.

How to relate these three realities remains a continuing challenge for all Christian theologians who take seriously the Church's deep-seated relationship with Judaism, myself included. At this point I cannot say that I have come to an entirely successful resolution of the matter. But I do know that I cannot be content with falling back into a perspective which says, as St. Paul did in Romans, that the solution remains a mystery known only to God. I feel compelled to continue to reflect on this matter and work toward some constructive resolution.

Two Christian biblical scholars, Walter Brueggemann and W.D. Davies, have been particularly helpful along this line. Their research and writings, coupled with Jewish reflections on the issue by Lawrence A. Hoffman,[11] Ruth Langer, Yehezkel Landau,[12] and others, have assisted theologians such as myself in framing the issue from a Christian standpoint.

As Brueggemann sees it, the central problem for Christian believers "is not emancipation but *rootage,* not meaning, but *belonging,* not separation from community but *location* within it, not isolation from others *but placement* deliberately between the generation of promise and fufillment."[13] Both the Hebrew Scriptures and the New Testament, Brueggemann maintains, present homelessness as a central human problem, and they seek to respond to it in terms of promise and gift. No truly believing Christian can avoid making land a central category in his or her belief system. On this point Brueggemann is unbending: "landed" faith is as much an imperative for Christians as for Jews.

W.D. Davies analyzes the required Christian appropriation of the biblical land tradition in somewhat greater detail than Brueggemann. He feels that, after all is said and done, the New Testament must be described as ambivalent on the land question, a view shared by another New Testament exegete long associated with the Jewish-Christian dialogue, John Townsend. In light of this, how Christians view the Hebrew Scriptures as a central resource for their faith perspective becomes crucial in terms of an approach to the land tradition in terms of the faith perspective of the Church.

Davies insists that there exist various strata within the New Testament that appear to take a critical approach to the land promises inherent in the Hebrew Scriptures. One passage, namely Acts 7, rejects them out of hand. However, there are other passages in which the land, the Temple, and Jerusalem in a clearly geographical sense are viewed in a quite positive light regarding their continued relevance for Christian self-identity. Davies's conclusion is that the New Testament leaves us with a twofold witness with respect to the land tradition. On the one hand, there is a sense in which faith in Christ takes the believer beyond the "confines" of the land of Israel, Jerusalem, and the Temple; yet, on the other, the New Testament's basic history and theology can never totally escape concern about these realities. For the New Testament writers, holy space exists wherever Christ is or has been. The Christ Event has universalized the land tradition of the Bible in a significant way, but not eliminated its centrality. Davies summarizes the impact of the Christ Event on the land tradition in this way:

> It (the New Testament) personalizes "holy space" in Christ, who, as a figure of history, is rooted in the land; he cleansed the Temple and died in Jerusalem, and lends his glory to these and to the places where he was, but, as Living Lord, he is also free to move wherever he wills. To do justice to the personalism of the New Testament, that is, to its Christocentricity, is to find the clue to the various strata of tradition that we have traced and to the attitudes they reveal: to their freedom from space, and their attachment to, spaces.[14]

A recent addition to this Christian discussion is the biblical scholar Richard Lux of the Sacred Heart School of Theology near Milwaukee. He is currently at work on a book on the subject. In this connection he has offered glimpses into his thinking in several recent lectures and in an article in the electronic journal *Studies in Christian-Jewish Relations*.[15] Lux builds his argument for the indispensable nature of the land tradition for Christian faith by focusing on the sacramental tradition in Catholic Christianity and applying it to the experience of a visit to the Holy Land for the Christian believer. For Lux the Holy Land has a strong potential for making Christ present to Christians. As Christians reimage their relationship to the Holy Land, according to Lux, they can assert that "As Christ is the sacrament of our encounter with God, the Holy Land is a sacrament of our encounter with Christ. . . . We can call this mediation of Christ in the Holy Land, a sacramental encounter; thus, the Holy Land, itself, becomes for us a sacramental experience."[16]

My own position is somewhat closer to that of Davies than to Brueggemann or Lux, though I share their commitment to Christian faith as "landed" faith. If I would have a question to address to Davies, it would be how he might relate the viewpoint expressed in the passage cited above to the perspective of some Jewish scholars such as Ellis Rivkin who have argued for a certain "universalization" of land and Temple as an integral element of the Pharisaioc reform during the Second Temple/Middle Judaic period.

In my judgment, dialogue with Judaism on the land question can greatly assist a recovery of "landed" faith in Christianity where such a notion has often been marginalized or totally pushed aside. It can help Christians see anew the need for expression of such a "landed" faith perspective in its prayer and worship. In Catholic Christianity the liturgical reforms of the eleven Vatican Council virtually eliminated any expression of a "landed" faith in its liturgical cycle.[17] That is why I believe Richard Lux is making an important contribution to the current discussion with his emphasis on the sacramentality of the land, even though I would part company with him in terms of an exclusive focus on Israel in terms of this sacramentality.

In terms of the renewed theology of Christian-Jewish bonding I would turn to model of Christianity and Judaism as following interrelated but distinctive paths to salvation. In such a perspective the biblical land tradition becomes a point of both of unity and a point of distinctiveness between Jews and Christians. Both traditions need to be rooted in the land. That is their point of agreement. But they are distinctive in terms of the territorial expression of that joint commitment. Nonetheless both have much to gain from an intense dialogue on the biblical land tradition.

Notes

1. Kittel, Gerhard and Gerhard Friedrick (eds.), *Theological Dictionary of the New Testament* (Grand Rapids, MI: Eerdmans, 1985).
2. Bea, Augustin Cardinal, *Church and the Jewish People: A Commentary on the Second Vatican Council's Declaration on the Relation of the Church to Non-Christian Religions.* Trans. by Philip Loretz (New York: Harper & Row, 1966).
3. On the Pope's meeting with Herzl, cf. Kertzer, David I., *The Popes Against the Jews: The Vatican's Role in the Rise of Modern Anti-Semitism* (New York: Knopf) 2001, 223 and Kreutz, Andrej, *Vatican Policy on the Palestinian-Israeli Conflict: The Struggle for the Holy Land* (Westport CT: Greenwood Press) 1990, 33. Also cf. Klein, Charlotte, "The Theological Dimensions of the State of Israel," *Journal of Ecumenical Studies* X:4 (Fall 1973): 704 and Coppa, Frank J., *The Papacy, the Jews, and the Holocaust* (Washington, DC: Catholic University of America Press, 2006) 107; 128-29.
4. Martyr, Justin, "Dialogue with Trypho," in *Fathers of the Church: Selections*, vol. 3, translated by Thomas B. Falls; revised and with a new Introduction by Thomas P. Halton. Edited by Michael Slusser (Washington, DC: Catholic University of America Press, 2003), #80.5.
5. Wilken, Robert, *The Land Called Holy* (New Haven, CT: Yale University Press, 1992), 58-59.
6. Bialer, Uri, *Cross on the Star of David: The Christian World in Israel's Foreign Policy, 1948-1967* (Bloomington/Indianapolis: Indiana University Press, 2005).
7. Paul II, Pope John, "Redemptionis Anno-Apostolic Letter on Jerusalem, *Origins*, 14:2 (May 24, 1984): 31-32.
8. Vatican Commission for Religious Relations with the Jews, "Notes on the Correct Way to Present Jews and Judaism in Preaching and Catechesis in the Roman Catholic Church,"

in Eugene J. Fisher and Leon Klenicki (eds.), *In Our Time: The Flowering of the Jewish-Catholic Dialogue* (New York/Mahwah, NJ: Paulist, 1990), #25.
9. Kenny, Anthony, *Catholics, Jews, and the State of Israel* (Mahwah, NJ: Paulist, 1993).
10. Langer, Ruth, "Theologies of the Land and the State: The Role of the Secular in Christian and Jewish Understandings," *Studies in Christian-Jewish Relations: An Electronic Journal*, 3 (2008), http://escholarship.bc.edu/scjr/vol3, 1-17.
11. Hoffman, Lawrence A., ed., *The Land of Israel: Jewish Perspectives* (Notre Dame, IN: University of Notre Dame Press, 1986).
12. Burrell, David and Yehezkel Landau (eds.), *Voices From Jerusalem: Jews and Christians Reflect on the Holy Land.* New York/Mahwah, NJ: Paulist, 1992; and Lawrence Boadt, CSP and Kevin di Camillo (eds.), *John Paul 11 in the Holy Land: In His Own Words with Christian and Jewish Perspectives by Yehezkel Landau and Michael McGarry, CSP* (New York/Mahwah, NJ: Paulist, 2001).
13. Brueggemann, Walter, *The Land* (Philadelphia: Fortress, 1977), 187.
14. Davies, W. D., *The Gospel and the Land* (Berkeley, CA: University of California Press, 1974), 367.
15. Lux, Richard, "The Land of Israel (Eretz Yisra'el) in Jewish and Christian Understanding," *Studies in Christian-Jewish Relations, An Electronic Journal,* 3:1 (2008), Article #4, http://escholarship.bc.edu/scjr/vol3, 1-18.
16. Ibid., 18.
17. Cf. Fragomeni, Richard N., "Liturgy at the Heart of Creation," and Edward Foley, Capuchin, Kathleen Hughes, RSCJ and Gilbert Ostdiek, OFM, "The Preparatory Rites: A Case Study in Liturgical Ecology," in Richard N. Fragomeni and John T. Pawlikowski (eds.), *The Ecological Challenge: Ethical, Liturgical and Spiritual Responses* (Collegeville, MN: The Liturgical Press, 1994), 67-82; 83-101.

THE PLACE OF "PLACE" IN JEWISH TRADITION

Nina Beth Cardin

Since the beginning of time, humans have had a problem with land. The first dilemma, of course, was the very mystery of land. That is, how did land itself, the ground we walk on, come into being? All relationship with and attitude toward the land would flow from this answer. The Torah addresses that problem with its opening line: God created the heavens and the earth.

That being the case, we can then conclude that God owns the land. All human claims to the land, therefore, are grounded in this basic knowledge. God first owned the land. It did not originally belong to us. Therefore, we must justify somehow any subsequent claim to use or ownership we may profess. But, how do we do that? What are our rights to the land? How are they earned? How conferred? How secured?

In addition we need to ask, even after justifying a claim to the land, what is the status of the land? Does this land/all land have a spiritual dimension? Or is it just a prop of life, a platform on which human history is played out? Can we do anything we want with it? Is it possible to lose our claim to land? If so, how? In which case what happens to the land? Does all land have the same meaning, or are some places different, holier, than others?

These questions about the status of land underlie the world's most pressing issues: political, economical and spiritual. They affect questions of property ownership and economic distribution of resources, environmental injustice, geopolitical warfare, resource and waste management, environmental ethics, and so on. And while Judaism is richly steeped in conversations on these subjects, with laws stipulating the proper use and distribution of land rights, the welfare of animals, appreciation of nature as witness to the majesty of God, etc., I am going to largely avoid these for the purposes of this paper and focus on the place of "place" in Jewish tradition.

As noted above, humans cannot ignore the experience and discourse of land. After all, we cannot exist without a place to be. All our experience is bound up with place. One of the first memories we recall about a remarkable or tragic event is where we were when it happened. Einstein's teacher, Hermann Minkowski, captured it succinctly when he said: "Nobody ever noticed a place except at a time, or a time except at a place." Jewish tradition, especially in its biblical stories, intimately combines event and place. Indivisible from the telling of our sacred history is the story of land itself. For the Jewish people, land is not just a backdrop, not a prop, but a partner, a covenantal character in our long unfolding sacred saga.

Cultures with autochthonous myths had it much easier. If the land spit you out, gave birth to you, you could claim that you belonged to that land, and that land belonged to you. (Remnants of this tradition remain in force even today. Citizenship is often determined not by parental status but by location at birth.) But a creation story that speaks of human beings created by God and then placed on the earth, or even created from the earth but not in a geographically identifiable or reclaimable spot, makes it problematic to claim possession and rights to a particular place. The Bible clearly wants to state that land is God's and any use or claim we humans make on it must be somehow divinely justifiable.

Even more, the story of the Jewish people begins with Abraham outside the land that his descendants would eventually call their own. Yet an enduring claim to a particular place is essential for a tradition like Judaism that is built on peoplehood. Even more telling, then, is the fact that the people were not born of, or in, the land. The Torah clearly wants to teach that no matter how central Israel:the land is to Israel:the people, occupancy in that land is a gift, not a given. The land belongs to God, and was gifted as part of the covenant, a dynamic component in a dynamic relationship of God, the people, Torah and the land.

The early chapters of the Torah seem bathed in this teaching. Chapter 1 of Genesis confers to the first humans the rights of usufruct over the whole earth, but ownership remains with God. From the perspective of Chapter 1, this seems more a matter of semantics than practical concern, for there are no other humans to challenge the first couple's claims, and no apparent boundaries to their "place." The distinction between use and ownership, then, while precise was inconsequential.

Chapters 2 and 3 spell out more clearly the human insecurity in relation to the land, both in the ability to call any place home and in being comfortably supported by it. (It is only in light of this Eden narrative that the verses in Chapter 1, specifically verses 26 and 28, can rear up and be much debated in environmental discussions of human rights and land ethics.)

In Chapter 4, Cain, the farmer, began the human experience of feeling alienated from the land. As punishment for killing Abel, the herder, Cain is told: "When you till the land, it shall not yield its goodness to you. A fugitive and wanderer shall you be on this earth" (Genesis 4:12). The land would harbor neither him nor his efforts at feeding himself. Even when Cain found a place to settle down, the Torah calls that place *Nod*—movement. Cain was the first of many generations of refugees who found the land inhospitable due to human aggression, whether their own aggression or the aggression of others.

The flood story, the Tower of Babel, even the call to Abraham to leave the place of his birth, broadcast the instability of the relationship between humans and their land.

Yet humans cannot live in such states of wandering, not knowing what place to call home, uncertain if where they got up in the morning will still be the place they can lay down that night. So, Abraham's call out of Ur was different from the previous biblical stories of displacement. Unlike the others, where displacement was punishment, this was redemption. It was not a separation from, but a calling to. Abraham was going home.

But that journey home for Abraham and his people has not been easy. It has not been a seamless, straightforward story of success. In that journey lies all the real-world problems of place as home.

For any people, the act of claiming any place is problematic. Do you claim it because no one got there before you? Do you claim it because you are stronger than those who are currently there? Do you claim it by building on it? Inheriting it? Planting it? Using it? Sticking a flag in its highest spot? Buying it?

Genesis 12 quite handily solves that problem for the Jewish people in perhaps the only way the Torah could: God gave the Jews that land. God made the earth; God owns the earth; God can gift the earth, or sections of it, to anyone God so chooses. And in this case, God chose to give the Jews that particular piece of land. While the precise contours and boundaries of the land may be open to question, the overall placement and claim to the land is neither questionable nor revocable. At least for generations of Jews.

For thousands of years, during the biblical golden age of Davidic settlement through the decades of the suffering of exile, the Jewish people turned to that place on earth called Judah, or Israel, or Zion, and knew it to be ours. Displacement or exile from the land never meant severance from the land, and certainly did not mean severance from our relationship with God. It meant rather deprivation of the land's immediate blessings, and was taken to be a sign that we had displeased God. But this was all absorbed amid a constant hope for reunion and restoration, and a continual spiritual and physical orientation to that place, Israel.

"By the waters of Babylon, there we sat down, and we wept... If I forget you, Jerusalem, let my right hand wither..." After the destruction of the Second Temple, throughout the second, 2,000-year-long exile, these words from Psalm 137 were recited as an introduction to the blessings said after weekday meals. But on Shabbat, the pain of exile was soothed by the dream of homecoming. The blessings after the festive meals on that day of rest were (and continue to be) introduced not with Psalm 137, but with Psalm 126, with the celebration of reunion: "When the Lord restores the grandeur of Zion—we can see it as in a dream—our mouths will be filled with laughter and our tongues with singing."

We might be far from home, the psalmist comforts us, we might be banished from the home God gave to us, but nonetheless, it is forever ours, and one day we will return.

Being far from home is a constant refrain in the stories of the Bible. What is notable is not just that the stories reflect a painful reality of Jewish history but they seem designed to reflect something more. Both the first part of *TaNaKh*, the Torah, and the last part of *TaNaKh*, the Writings, end their storytelling at the boundaries of homecoming, with the promise of return, the taste of return, but not the experience of return. Why could the Torah not end with the first chapters of Joshua? Why could Chronicles not end with the Jews returning to their land? Why would the editors of the Bible choose to frame these sacred texts in terms of promise instead of arrival?

Perhaps that is part of the rich wisdom of our tradition, where particularistic history intersects with universal experience. Such an expression of expectant homecoming is spiritual metaphor for the constant hope that keeps each of us alive, individually and collectively, as we struggle with the angst of existential wandering. What indeed is the purpose of our lives? Where in fact is that ultimate place called home? What is our purpose here? Where are we going? Where do we really belong? No doubt that is one reason these stories maintain their resonance and claim on us all these years, for they speak on multiple levels of truth.

But this nod to the universal does not cancel out the particular. Nor does the awareness of the sometimes ephemeral connection to home dilute our passion and commitment to homeland.

For the Jewish people, our life, our calendar, our holidays, our liturgy, our stories, our orientation (the way we build our synagogues, decorate our homes, and turn our bodies when we pray), are all bound up in that particular bit of land on the east coast of the Mediterranean Sea. To this day, if we live outside the land, we might decorate our walls with art from Israel, or mark the wall that faces Jerusalem, purchase goods from there, send *tzedakah*, donations, there, and seek to be buried with dirt from there.

And yet, we have always acknowledged that Jews can have a "place" outside of Israel. Even before we reached there (Numbers 32), portions of the Jewish people petitioned to live east of the Promised Land. "Now, the children of Reuben and the children of Gad had a great deal of cattle. And they saw that the land of Jazer and the land of Gilead was a good place for cattle...so they spoke to Moses and Eliezer the priest and the heads of the assembly...and said, 'If we have found favor in your eyes, let this land be given to us for a possession...'"

At first this was seen as blasphemy, treachery, a disassociation from the Jewish people. Living outside the land meant living outside the people. But the renegade tribes argued, no, not at all. While "we will build sheepfolds here for our cattle and cities for our little ones, we ourselves will be armed to go to battle with the children of Israel until we have brought them to their place... We will not return to our houses until every family in Israel has inherited their inheritance."

Jews may choose to live outside the land, indeed may prefer to live outside the land. But that does not break our bonds with our people, or break the bonds of peoplehood and homeland.

I would argue that the tradition of placing a *mezuzah* on every Jewish home is an expression of this sense of extended shared residence. The *mezuzah* is a visual marker placed on the doorpost of a Jewish house. It holds within it a portion of the Torah text. This marker transforms the Jewish home into an embassy of the Holy Land. These homes may be discontiguous in space but they are bound to the specific places of each other, and to the central place of Israel, Even more, they are bound to each other *through* the central place of Israel. The mezuzah also emphasizes the spiritual dimension of Israel, above and beyond its geophysical dimension. For as long as Israel is grounded in real time and place, its spiritual dimensions can reach beyond its physical boundaries.

This connection works in both directions. The primacy of home in Israel is never diminished. Our rootedness and security are bound up in the land and landscape of Israel. That is our source, the hub and hearth that grounds us and warms us. And yet, the boundaries of home are not barriers. Teachings, wisdom, people, and God's presence flow from there to here, filling the world. The rabbis called the synagogue *mikdash me'at*, the diminutive Holy Place, the surrogate Temple. While the Temple and Jerusalem can never be replaced or supplanted, emanations of their sacredness can be felt around the world.

Here is another tidbit to add to the complexity of "place." Despite the entire Torah focusing on getting the Jewish people to the Promised Land, we do not mark, remember or celebrate the moment of our reentry. It is not that we do not know when it happened. "And the people came up out of the Jordan on the tenth day of the first month, and encamped at Gilgal..." (Joshua 4:19). This is the crossing of the Jewish people from the centuries of slavery into the promised land. This is the moment the people had been waiting for. This was the moment that Moses was not able to see. Yet neither the *TaNaKh* nor the rabbis ever stipulate that we celebrate this date. It is not noted in our schools nor is this portion read annually in our synagogue cycle. Despite the fact that two full chapters are given over to describe this crossing, this date was never codified in the Jewish sacred calendar.

Perhaps this lack of interest is meant to downplay the militaristic aspect of reclaiming the land; indeed, to downplay any people's militaristic desire to claim any land by force. Perhaps the Bible and the rabbis wanted to stress that Israel's claim to the land was not dependent on its wartime successes but rather on the age-old gifting of the land by God to Abraham. Perhaps the intentional oversight of this date is to stress that despite the Joshua narratives no [other] military success is sufficient to claim ownership of any land.

And yet we cannot avoid the need to claim land. Particularity of land ownership is essential, even while it is wildly problematic and the source of strife and killing throughout the generations of humankind. The *TaNaKh* seems to struggle with balancing the need and the challenge, human ownership with the truth that only God is the land's true owner. The laws of the Jubilee, the return of all land transfers every fifty years to the "original" tribal owner is one way the biblical tradition manages these conflicting needs. The imposed seventh year of rest for the land, the *shemittah* year or *shevi'it*, is another.

At various places in the biblical literature, the land of Israel given to the Jewish people is called *nahalah*. *Nahalah* is a word that refers to a section of a great swath of land owned by a master/progenitor that is given as an inheritance or gift to child or inheritor. Both the land of Israel for the Jews, and the Jewish people to God, are called *nahalah*. From this we can learn that all the earth's land is of a piece, created and blessed by God. But discrete areas of land are gifted, and needed, by discrete peoples and nations. This seems to be the best way the Bible can manage this complex and problematic question of "place."

All land is *eretz*, therefore, God's creation. All people are *bnei adam*, humanity. All people will need a place to claim as their own. For the Jewish people, Israel:the land is believed to be covenantly and eternally bound to Israel:the people. And both are covenantly and eternally bound to God.

MEET THE NEW PAUL, SAME AS THE OLD PAUL
Michael Wychograd, Kendall Soulen, and the New Problem of Supersessionism

William Plevan

I had the privilege of meeting both Kendall Soulen and Michael Wyschograd at a conference sponsored by the Institute for Christian-Jewish Studies in Baltimore. ICJS had gathered a group of Jewish and Christian (all from Presbyterian and Lutheran backgrounds) scholars, clergy, educators and lay people to participate in six study and dialogue sessions over the course of two years on the subject of "The Scandal of Particularity." The aim of the series was to engage a variety of stakeholders in the future of Jewish-Christian relations by examining the question of how our different traditions conceive of their own particularity, and how expressions of particularity impact the way we understand our involvement in the public square of American political and social life and our relations with members of other faith traditions. Rather than limit interfaith dialogue by hoping to find some kind of "common ground" shared by Judaism and Christianity, the conference dared us to think that the differences between these two traditions might be more important than any similarities we might find, and that these supposed similarities might be superficial at best.

Soulen and Wyschograd could not have been a better pair to bring as guest scholars to the ICJS conference. This is partly because Wyschograd has been one of the leading Jewish participants in Jewish-Christian dialogue in the past forty years, and Soulen has been his most important Christian admirer and interpreter. More significantly, it is because of the way both Wyschograd and Soulen have dealt with the issue of particularity in their work on the theological relationship between Judaism and Christianity. In his seminal work, *The Body of Faith*, Wyschograd argued that the central theological concept of Judaism is God's election of Israel to be God's beloved people. While God demands that Israel observe the commandments and while certain beliefs about God's nature may be implicit in the Biblical record, the essence of divine election is not the commandments or any beliefs about God, but rather God's preferential and parental love of the carnal family of Israel, the flesh and blood decedents of Jacob.

One of the most refreshing aspects of Wyschograd's Jewish theology is his open acknowledgment that those aspects of Christian theology that Jews typically find most un-Jewish, like the incarnation of God in Jesus Christ, actually have roots in Jewish ideas, such as God's presence in the people Israel. This willingness to reject simplistic dichotomies between Judaism and Christianity has greatly enriched interfaith dialogue, as it did for us at the conference. Indeed, Wyschograd's philosophical and theological work has always been concerned with the relationship between Judaism and Christianity, and he acknowledges his debt to Christian thinkers, particularly Kierkegaard and Karl Barth, not only for his understanding of Christianity but also for his understanding of Judaism as a religion of carnal election.

Because of his serious and open-minded engagement with Christianity, Wyschograd has also been influential in both academic and theological circles for his novel interpretations of the epistles of the Apostle Paul. Paul is often viewed by Jewish critics as the father of supersessionism for supposedly rejecting the validity of the commandments of the Torah after the death and resurrection of Jesus Christ. It is this interpretation of Paul that formed the basis for the Church's claim that God has rejected the Jews for their rejection of Christ and made the Church the "new Israel," the inheritors of God's preferential love. And it is precisely this interpretation of Paul that Wyschograd challenges, suggesting instead that Paul not only maintains that the commandments have validity for Jews but also that Paul believes that Israel's covenant with God is never abrogated. Centuries of Christian theologians have, according to Wyschograd, been misreading Paul. This new reading, sometimes dubbed "the New Paul," undermines two millennia of theological rationales for Christian supersessionism.

Although I am not a scholar of the New Testament, and hence unwilling to claim an authoritative judgment, I do find the basic elements of the New Paul reading convincing, some reasons for which I will indicate below. As I learned at the conference by watching a particularly intense exchange between Soulen and another New Testament scholar, the New Paul reading, like most scholarly paradigms, has many variations, some much more radical than what I presented above and all with significant implications for Christian theology and Jewish-Christian relations. What I wish to do here, is to ask to what extent the New Paul reading has overcome the problem of supersessionism in Christian theology. To do this I will briefly examine Kendell Soulen's critique of supersessionism in Christian theology and then ask whether we might still learn something from Martin Buber's interpretation of Paul that can lead us to see a new problem of supersessionism that lies deep at the heart of Paul's rhetoric on the law.

That the new Paul reading does take us very far in ridding Christianity of its supersessionist tendencies is at the heart of Kendall Soulen's theological work. In his introduction to a collection of Wyschograd's essays that he edited, Soulen explains that he himself first became acquainted with Wyschograd in the context of trying to understand Paul's letter to the Romans, chapters 9-11. These chapters are critical for the New Paul reading, because it is here that Paul discusses the fate of God's covenant with Israel and states clearly (Rom. 11:1-2) that God has not rejected Israel, and seems to imply that this is so even for Jews who reject Christ. The heart of supersessionism—the idea that the Church has supplanted Israel as the bearer of a covenantal relationship with God and that Israel has been spurned for its rejection of Christ—is severely undercut by these passages. In his important book, *The God of Israel and Christian Theology*, Soulen devotes only a few pages to discussing these passages in Paul, but this is misleading, as that entire book should be understood as the theological outgrowth of the new reading of Paul for which Wyschograd may be considered the founding father. The essence of Wyschograd's reading, then, is that Paul grasps and affirms what he, Wyschograd, takes to be the central theological teaching of the Hebrew Bible: that God's carnal election of Israel is irrevocable, that God's promises to the children of Abraham will be fulfilled, and that God's commandments to the Jewish people remain eternally valid.

Wyschograd maintains that his reading of Paul suggests that no matter how one interprets the apostle's negative rhetoric about "the law" as "a curse" that brings sin into the world, Paul himself maintained his observance of the commandments and thought other Jews should as well. The strongest case for this claim is perhaps the debate in Acts 15 between those who required and those (Paul included) who did not require the observance of the commandments *for Gentiles*. The debate assumes, Wyschograd suggests, that all involved, Paul included, took it for granted that the commandments remained obligatory *for Jews*. Indeed, Paul's negative rhetoric about the law appears largely in his two epistles, Romans and Galatians, that are missives in the same debate: whether Gentiles needed to convert to Judaism in order benefit from Christ's redemptive acts. This aspect of the New Paul reading leads Wyschograd to suggest that the Church has erred in viewing the commandments as either a curse for the Jews for their sinfulness or as merely pre-figuring Christ's arrival and in teaching that Jewish converts to Christianity should cease observing the commandments of the Torah. In a famous letter to the French Catholic Cardinal Lustiger, Wyschograd insists that the Cardinal, born a Jew, should himself observe the commandments, which would mark a return to the theological understanding of the early church. This view certainly sounds strange to contemporary Jewish ears as well, and both Wyschograd and Soulen, somewhat controversially, have advised congregations of Jewish Christians (sometimes known as "Messianic Jews") on their need to maintain their obedience to the Torah's commandments.

This novel understanding of how Christianity should view the validity of the commandments of the Torah may be the most striking feature of Soulen's critique of Christian theology, but it follows from his claim that Christian theology must place the Hebrew Bible at the center of its understanding of God's relationship with humanity. In *The God of Israel and Christian Theology*, Soulen argues that supersessionism has actually been a great burden to Christian theology. While Soulen is hardly the first Christian to call for the end of supersessionist rhetoric or Christian triumphalism against Jews and Judaism (not to mention overt anti-Semitism), his book is a thorough and penetrating analysis of the problems that arise within Christian theology as a result of its supersessionist structure. The essential problem of theological supersessionism, as

Soulen identifies it deep in the sources of Christian theology, is the claim that Israel's experience with its God does not teach Christians anything about how God acts in human history. While ignoring God's enduring concern for Israel, Christian theology has been insufficiently attentive to the theological implications of God's involvement in Israel's national life as recorded in the Hebrew Bible. The result is that Christian theology has been inadequate in delineating and explaining the public and historical aspects of the life of Christian faith. Without the embodied covenantal life of Israel as its backdrop, Christianity must rely on metaphysical and individualist strategies for interpreting and developing the message of the Gospel.

In Soulen's analysis, the story that Christian theology has told since the first century begins with the creation of humanity and its descent into sin as recorded in the opening chapters of Genesis, only to skip the entire history of Israel and pick up at the life, death and resurrection of Jesus Christ, whose sacrifice brings redemption from sin. Thus, Christian theology has been woefully inadequate in understanding God's role as *consummator*, or as a God who promises to bring about the perfection of creation through the perfection of humanity. Christian theology has historically, Soulen shows, viewed God's consummation of humanity as put on hold after the fall and until the redemptive life of Jesus Christ. But if Christianity is to truly view its God as the same God of Israel, then it must view God's covenantal history with Israel as part of God's consummating work. And this consummating work is not only for Israel, but for the nations as well, who, as God promised to Abraham, would be blessed through his descendents.

Soulen's concerns about Christian theology's historically limited view about God's role as consumator was evident in a discussion that he and I had at the ICJS conference over lunch. The issue concerned his reading of Genesis 1:27-8, in which God pronounces that the human being should be created in the divine image and shall rule over creation. Soulen claimed in his presentation at the conference that this verse on its own was not a sufficient account of God's plan for humanity's perfection. In our discussion, I took the opposite view, namely that the verse contains the key for understanding humanity role in divine creation. In my view, humanity's dominion over creation assumes that human beings are capable of recognizing ultimate divine rule over creation, and that their role is to be, to use the rabbinic phrase, partners with God in perfecting creation. Indeed, on the Bible's view, early humans, as much as they fall into destructive patterns of violence of corruption, are aware, apparently without the benefit of special divine revelation, of the presence of God to whom they offer sacrifices and desire to know and approach.

I am not persuaded to change my mind on this point, but a more careful reading of Soulen's book has allowed me to appreciate that his reading is meant to deflect the kind of Christian inattentiveness to the role of God as consummator in the *rest* of the Hebrew Bible. In this respect, I agree with Soulen that the Hebrew Bible as a whole continues the story of God's role in the perfection of creation, and hence is more than just a story about Israel's redemption. Moreover, Soulen's insight into the deep blind spot of Christian theology has made me wonder whether my own view on Genesis 1:27-8 reflects a kind of Jewish blind spot as well. For if Christians have historically ignored God's relationship with the people Israel in understanding God's role as consummator, it is not possible that Jews have historically ignored God's relationship with the nations in understanding God's role as redeemer? If Jews are to take this possibility seriously, then we cannot limit our understanding of God's relationship to the nations of the world to the first eleven pre-Abrahamic chapters of Genesis. Indeed, this seems to be precisely the warning the prophet Amos delivers when he reminds Israel that God also acted to bring other nations of the world from one land to another as God did for Israel (Amos 9:7).

Soulen's claim that the Hebrew Bible teaches something of relevance to all of humanity about the relationship between God and God's creation has a long Jewish pedigree. This idea was particularly favored by modern European-Jewish thinkers who felt compelled to defend Judaism's cultural and religious value to both Jews and non-Jews who viewed Judaism as an ossified faith. One such thinker, Martin Buber, actually wrote a major study of the New Testament arguing that Christianity's rejection of the Hebrew Bible as a source for Christianity is rooted in the writings of the apostle Paul himself. Thus, while Buber and Soulen share a great deal in their view of the Hebrew Bible, they differ sharply on how to interpret Paul. And while in most respects I think Soulen and Wyschograd's readings of Paul are more convincing than Buber's, I hope to show how Buber's reading of Paul draws our attention to some aspects of Paul's view of the law that I think are not sufficiently treated by Wyschograd and Soulen and suggest what I am calling the new problem of supersessionism.

Buber is widely regarded as the Jewish thinker with the greatest affinity with Christian thought, and many assume that this affinity is due to Buber's rejection of the authority of rabbinic law. But in his study of the New Testament *Two Types of Faith*, Buber acknowledges not an affinity with Christianity but an appreciation of the teachings of the "real" or "historical" Jesus of Nazareth, which he distinguishes from the teachings of Paul and the later Church. Buber's Jesus is a teacher in the tradition of the Biblical prophets, whom for Buber are the most spiritually authentic voice in the Hebrew Bible and the genuine founders of Judaism. Buber argued that the central religious idea of the prophetic tradition was that Israel was commanded to realize the kingship of God, which he understood as the creation of a concrete community which realizes holiness and righteousness in its everyday, embodied existence, working for the day when God would eventually perfect creation. Buber's Judaism is not a spiritualization of Jewish teaching, but a focus on the realization of holiness in concrete communal life. Jesus' teaching about the coming of the reign of God was not, in Buber's view, a departure from this Biblical religion but an attempt at its realization.

Soulen's own retrieval of the Hebrew Bible emphasizes precisely this prophetic idea of the reign of God. Soulen says that correcting the lack of attention to the Hebrew Bible in Christian theology requires "a frank reorientation of the hermeneutical center of the Scriptures from the incarnation to the reign of God, where God's reign is understood as the eschatological outcome of human history at the end of time" (GI 138). Whereas Christian theology has traditionally read the incarnation of God in the person of Jesus Christ as marking the end of God's covenantal history with Israel, the heart of the supersessionist claim, Soulen argues that the incarnation is the proclamation that God's promises to Israel will be fulfilled *as Israel*, that is with Israel maintaining its integrity and distinctiveness from the gentile nations, who of course will also be included in God's reign.

Both Buber and Soulen also contend that Christianity's turn away from the core of the Hebrew Bible represents a form of latent Gnosticism, or semignosticism. Yet, they develop this idea in significantly different ways that bears on their differing views of Paul. Gnosticism was the movement that declared that the God Jesus claimed as "Father" was different than the God of Israel depicted in the Hebrew Bible. For Gnostics, the teachings of Jesus have nothing at all to do with the Biblical God, who is merely a demonic demiurge. As an official matter, the early Church rejected Gnosticism, and the early Church fathers, as Soulen describes in his book, engaged in polemical debates with Gnostics about the continuity of the teachings of Jesus with those of the Hebrew Bible as much as they did with Jews and pagans. But Soulen thinks that the departure from Gnosticism did not go far enough, as the hermeneutical product of this effort only took the opening chapters of Genesis seriously in order to understand God's consummating work. Since the early Church, Soulen concludes, the Hebrew Bible has been only a little more valuable to Christians as a source for understanding God's consummating work as it was for the Gnostics.

Buber saw the potential for a latent Gnosticism in Christian theology first hand as many German theologians, some of whom were not even anti-Semitic, in the early twentieth century began to question the relevance of the Hebrew Bible and Jesus' Jewish roots for understanding Christian teaching. In the nineteen-thirties with the rise of National Socialism, Buber drew an explicit connection between the denigration of the Hebrew Bible in Christian Theology and the denigration of the Jewish people in Christian Europe. Buber also saw the latent Gnosticism in Christianity as having an ontological component, which Soulen does not. By this Buber means that Christianity, on his view, goes a long way to adopting the Gnostic teaching that the human spirit can only be realized, or achieve holiness, by escaping the concrete world of material existence. In *Two Types of Faith*, Buber argues that while Jesus' teaching was consistent with the Biblical tradition of thinking of holiness and the human spirit as realized in embodied, concrete existence, the apostle Paul, as well as the Gospel according to John is deeply influenced by Gnostic teachings about the nature of the holiness. Buber's title refers to the Biblical type of faith that he thinks Jesus and the early Pharisees both exemplified, as opposed to the Gnostic type of faith that emphasized intellectual belief in an unseen reality that Paul, later Christianity and some philosophical and mystical strands of later Judaism exemplified.

Buber sees the strongest evidence for the Gnostic influence on Paul in the apostle's rhetoric on "the law," by which Paul seems to mean the commandments of the Torah. Interestingly, Buber, like Wyschograd, acknowledges that Paul thought the law ought to be observed, at least by Jews. Given that Buber himself disregarded the authority of rabbinic law (halakha), there is no need to wonder whether his opposition to Pauline teaching was rooted in a defense of Jewish "legalism"; Buber himself opposed such legalism. Yet, in Paul's rhetoric about the curses associated with the law, Buber detects the latent ontological Gnosticism Soulen does not find at all in Christian sources. In Buber's view, Paul thinks that the Torah "was given not in order to be fulfilled but rather through its incapability of fulfillment to call forth sin 'in order that it might abound'" (TTF 80). On Buber's interpretation, even though Paul calls the law "holy" and "spiritual" (Rom. 7:12,14), he is teaching is that the Biblical program of realizing what Buber calls "holiness in the everyday" is not achievable, and that the commandments were given to prove precisely its very impossibility, which then paves the way for redemption from sin through Jesus Christ.

Soulen's entire project of correcting the supersessionist tendencies of Christian theology may be viewed as a direct response to Buber's claim of latent Gnosticism or semignosticism in Paul. Soulen's argument, as I understand it, is that by attending to God's work of consummation in economy of mutual blessing between Israel and the nations, Christian theology can provide an accurate account for the way discipleship in Christ takes shape in public, embodied existence, which counters any possible interpretation that would align Christianity with ontological Gnosticism. Paul, as understood by the New Paul reading, is marshaled as a resource for this argument by showing that Paul rejects neither the corporeal election of the Jewish people nor the authority of the commandments.

I think that Wyschograd and Soulen's reading of Paul on this point is ultimately more persuasive than Buber's. As I noted above, one of Wyschograd's important contributions to *Jewish* theology is that he is willing to recover the carnality of Biblical thought that he believes had been discarded in order to distinguish Judaism from Christian incarnationalism. Thus, Wyschograd acknowledges the carnality of later Christian theology that Buber seems to ignore. In Wyschograd's view, the dominant Christian teaching is that holiness is realized carnally, in a body, and at the highest level by Jesus Christ, God incarnated in a human body. What Christianity had historically done, however, was to deny the holiness of the people Israel, by claiming they have been rejected by God for their rejection of Jesus. Wyschograd's reading of Paul comes to show that the apostle himself refused this approach, and Soulen shows how the obscuring of this critical detail has had disastrous consequences for Christian teaching. And if Soulen and Wyschograd are correct about Paul, then Soulen is probably also correct that ontological Gnosticism was never as big a temptation for Christian theology as Buber thought.

But even if Buber did overstate the latent ontological Gnosticism in Paul and later Christian teaching, his central insight about Paul's view of the law is worth considering. Indeed, even if Paul believes the law is valid, he also thinks that it is insufficient for realizing holiness. Moreover, Paul treats the gift of Torah to Israel as a kind of divine ruse. Israel's carnal election may be eternal, but for what end? If it is merely to teach the world about the persistence of sinfulness, then what can be said about the actual role of Israel in the economy of consummation and redemption? Is it merely to live under the curse of the law until the arrival of the law of grace through the life of Jesus Christ? Attending to Paul's view of the law then raises the question of whether supersessionism does not in fact have deep roots in Paul, even if the Church misunderstood certain significant aspects of Paul's claims. Additionally, Paul's view of the law as a kind of instrument of divine preparation points to what I think of the new problem of supersessionism.

If the old problem of supersessionism was the idea that Israel's role in the economy of consummation and redemption has been completely usurped by the Church, then the new problem of supersessionism is whether the commandments of the Torah are of intrinsic or merely instrumental value in fulfilling Israel's historic role. Even if Buber rejected the authority of the entire rabbinic legal system, what he shares with most modern Jewish religious thinkers, including Wyschograd, but also Rosenzweig, Heschel, and Soloveitchik, is that God's covenant with Israel demands action, the end of which is the realization of a holy community, and that a holy community through its action can play a role in the redemption of the world. Buber believed that this was the central teaching of the Biblical prophets and the Hasidic masters, as well as that of Jesus and the Pharisees. Paul's rhetoric of the law seems to suggest that at the very least he did not think that Israel's performance of the commandments on their own would create a truly holy community. Only with the benefit of grace in Christ, and recognizing the insufficiency of the law in bringing about grace, could any member of the house of Israel meaningfully participate in the economy of consummation and redemption.

The ancient Israelite community and every subsequent generation of Jewish thinkers have recognized that mechanical observance of the law is insufficient to bringing about holiness. Likewise human beings, being flawed mortals, were unlikely to observe the commandments perfectly. The Hebrew Bible's solution to the problem of human frailty is to offer the possibility for human beings to be cleansed of their sins and achieve reconciliation with God. In Biblical religion, that process of reconciliation is enacted in the institution of the Tabernacle and the sacrificial cult, which become the basis for the Temple in Jerusalem. The Temple is not merely a place of worship, it is the point of access to the spirit of the divine presence, which not only cleanses Israel but all of humanity for its sins, allowing the gift of divine blessing to radiate to the entire world.

I think it is worth remembering that Paul's ministry was carried out while the second Temple still stood, and it is worth asking what Paul speeches about the law mean in light of this historical detail. Whatever the historical relationship between Jesus and his early followers and other Jewish groups like the Essenes who rejected the contemporary Temple hierarchy, it seems clear that the early Church did not see the locus of divine holiness in the currently standing Temple. Paul's view of the law seems to reflect this rejection, because for him the spirit of God's holiness is only available through the person of Jesus Christ. It is possible that when Paul speaks of the law, he does not mean those commandments related either to the sacrificial cult or those that are explicitly related to the inculcation of holiness, such as dietary restrictions and the Sabbath. But even if he does, he has, it would seem, definitively concluded that the Temple ceased to be effective in bringing the spirit of God to the people of Israel and the world.

Soulen's treatment of the Hebrew Bible rightly emphasizes what he calls the "economy of mutual blessing" between Israel and the nations that is at the heart of the Biblical theological narrative. It is for this reason that the absence of any discussion of the holy tabernacle or the later Temple in Jerusalem in God's dealings with the people Israel is so startling. In the Hebrew Bible, the Temple cult is the exclusive medium of divine blessing not only for Israel but for the world as well. Israel's maintenance of the Temple cult and other strictures of bodily holiness allows for God to find a dwelling, literally a home, not only within Israel, but in the world. Such a dwelling allows God to bestow blessing not only on Israel, but for that blessing to extend to the four corners of the earth. The messianic hope expressed by the Israelite prophets is that the nations of the world would come to Jerusalem and worship at this Temple; but their current failure to do so did not prevent their receiving the benefit of the divine blessing that emanated from there.

The significance of the Temple for late ancient Judaism was such that its destruction stimulated a monumental crisis for the most pious Jews of that generation, and the urgent sense of loss at the Temple's destruction became a central feature of classical rabbinic Judaism. Wyschograd's theology of carnal election is Biblically centered, but it also reflects the rabbinic response to the Temple's destruction by asserting that God not only continues to love Israel despite the destruction but also that God's holiness works through God's election of Israel *for the sake of the world*. As I remarked, Paul's writing already show a lack of interest in the fate of the Temple and the holiness that flowed to Israel as a result. This may be the most un-Jewish aspect of Paul's Christianity: the utter lack of concern for the religion of the Temple. And the most supersessionist aspect of Christian theology may not be the claim of Jesus as Messiah or as Jesus as the incarnation of God, but Jesus as a sacrifice, or the final sacrifice. This, I believe, is where our discussion of supersessionism should continue.

THE SCANDAL OF PARTICULARITY
Particularity and the Public Square

Paul D. Hanson

A personal note

Thank you for the opportunity to join your exploration of the Scandal of Particularity, specifically as it focuses on Particularity and the Public Square. David Novak may share my sense of being a *ger* who has passed over a border, entered a very special land, and been welcomed as a member of your extended family. Your gracious hospitality notwithstanding, I am aware that you have developed bonds of kinship and understanding, the nature and depth of which are unknown to me, even as my own *nephesh* in large part is unknown to you. Out of my desire to move from the alienation of the stranger toward the communion of a fellow pilgrim on the fascinating journey you have been taking, I am going to share a few thoughts regarding my faith tradition and the bearing it has on the over-arching theme of your Joint Project, particularly its starting point in the challenge presented by the "erosion of center."

I understand my faith in terms of a specific historical ontology. My identity, my very being, arises out of a relationship with God chronicled in the Hebrew and Christian Scriptures, amplified through a long history of interpretation by rabbis and theologians, and extended to me in a most personal and intimate way by Christian parents within the context of a Lutheran Church that they cherished and supported. The tiny town on the south shore of Lake Superior in which I spent my first seventeen years was unfamiliar with the phenomenon of religious and cultural diversity as it is experienced in most regions of the country today. The

Italian and Polish miners attended St. Joseph's Parish, the Swedish and Finnish foresters attended First Lutheran. There were no people of dark skin in Wakefield, though there was one Jewish merchant. Prejudice against minorities was not blatant, but to deny its latency in our Sunday school materials and the jokes people shared around the dinner table would be tantamount with resigning oneself to a life of bigotry.

Fortunately for me, my life has been a journey of border crossings, on which the ignorance that matures into prejudice has been dismantled, one personal encounter at a time: Isaiah Mbang at Gustavus Adolphus College, Tim Lim at Yale Divinity School, Buzzy Fishbane at Harvard University, and on and on. The challenges were not only cultural, they were religious. But unlike the repudiation of a faith tradition that was so common among my academic peers, encounter led me not to renunciation of my ancestral faith, but to a deepened understanding of that faith. That background lies at the heart of my present work on religion and politics. The theo-political hermeneutic with which I work is simply an extension of an ongoing life-journey, a stage in the development of my historical ontology.

I invite you now to visit with me a very personal moment in my life-journey that hopefully will help you to understand my personal relation to the problem of the "erosion of center." We are strolling along the shore of a cove in the Penobscott Bay in Maine, my wife Cynthia, my daughter Amy, my sons Mark and Nathaniel, their spouses and their little ones, my precious grandchildren. This happens every July, this gathering of our family, our *mišpaḥah*. The significance of this primal community in my self-understanding is described by David Novak in "The Jewish Political Contract."[1] As I mentioned earlier, my identity, my being is the creation of a millennia-long relationship, and I cannot begin to trace the genealogy that preserved faithfully the understanding of a compassionate God through persecution, intellectual assault, and the seduction of assimilation so as to bless me with the key to my understanding of life as gift and responsibility.

That sense of heritage at my mature stage in life is the source of profound joy alloyed with a tinge of sorrow. Why this mixture of feelings? Amy, my oldest, and her husband Gary Tatz, the son of an Orthodox Rabbi, are raising Gabriel and Joshua in a family overflowing with parental love and deep compassion toward the underserved, but without congregational participation in either Judaism or Christianity. Mark, my middle child, and his Armenian/Ukranian wife Christina are raising Nicholas and Christopher within the covenant relationship of a Presbyterian congregation combining faithfulness to the Gospel with commitment to social justice. Nathaniel, my youngest, and his wife Casey have left their Lutheran and Catholic past and are unaffiliated as they raise their children, Lily and Winslow, within the tenderness and intimacy of a truly remarkable family and on the basis of high moral standards.

As I see my offspring and their offspring skipping and laughing and playing along sands and stones deposited on our shoreline over geological ages, I thank God for the most exquisite gift I can imagine, my most enduring legacy, children and grandchildren. But I would be less than truthful if I did not acknowledge sadness evoked by thoughts such as, "What will be the effects of two of my three children severing the thread that had been preserved over the generations of Cynthia's and my ancestors that enables us to inherit such rich blessings? Did we fail to tutor them in teachings of our faith, in spite of our life-long involvement in our Lutheran community? Were we defective in manifesting the relevance of that faith for our daily lives, especially in relation to the underserved and the oppressed?" Excluded from our thinking was any religious pedagogy other than trusting their sacred right to decide for themselves what their personal relation to our ancestral tradition would be. Yet, since I embrace not only the beauty but also the truth of my biblical tradition, I feel something has been lost that has implications for the enormous moral challenges facing our world in generations to come. Please do not misunderstand me, Amy and Gary and Casey, serving the sick and outcast as medical doctors, and Nathaniel, bracketing his own professional career to nurture Lily and Winslow, are upholding human values that make parents proud, but..., but..., is something eroding in an ontological foundation that will have long-ranging effects far beyond our life-spans? And as you have been observing in your work together, what I have described is not limited to one family, but is widespread throughout our culture, affecting Jews and Christians alike.

A fashionable solution

There is no need to sketch a taxonomy of alternatives available in our society for those facing the challenge of relating their religious tradition to modernity. But I shall refer to one fashionable solution as a means of introducing my own thoughts on the issue of the scandal of particularity as it relates to the public square.

We all know Jewish/Christian couples who have found as the fair-minded solution to their religious differences the middle ground offered by the Unitarian Universalist Association. The UUA is perhaps the religious paragon of American pragmatism. Faced with the scandal of religious particularity, two individuals locate middle ground in an association whose "dogma" is the eschewal of explicit confessions and beliefs. As one of their bumper stickers declares, "UUA, Where the Question is the Answer." Would the prospects for civil harmony and international peace be enhanced if all religions adopted this lowest common denominator policy, leading to a liberal-democratic "overlapping consensus"? That has been the rationale of the Civil Religion phenomenon in America. But its long-term adequacy for preserving the foundational values of a society is questionable.

Unitarians represent a very constructive intellectual and moral force in our society, advocating for justice and equality and respecting the rights of others to believe as they choose. Not so with the atheistic philosopher Richard Dawkins, who declares categorically that belief in God is a delusion that detracts from the shared human task of maintaining a decent world on the basis of science and reason. Though finding in the contemporary world an intelligent, sharp-tongued spokesperson whose book *The God Delusion* has sold close to two million copies, the theory that religion has exercised a deleterious effect on human civilization is nothing new, and the evidence elicited has included everything from the wars of Joshua to the Muslim conquests of the seventh and eighth centuries to the medieval Crusades. Within our own time, those who support this theory draw attention to the bellicose position of some Fundamentalists toward minorities at home and religious communities abroad that they see abetting what Samuel Huntington has called "a clash of civilizations."[2]

The case for the positive role of religious particularity in a religiously and culturally diverse society

The case for a positive role for religious communities that do not deny but publically affirm and enact their particular beliefs and practices in society must begin with acknowledgment of the fact that religious particularity often has been abused as an instrument of repression of minorities and hatred toward adherents of different worldviews. This starting point places several obligations on the community claiming that faithfulness to its beliefs and practices and public testimony to its principles represent a valuable moral resource for the maintenance of a just and humane society, a resource that is not replicated by but is fully capable of cooperating with other moral agencies.

The first obligation is to foster a communal identity as a people created by a loving God, called into a covenant relationship with God, and committed to obey God as the only *ultimate* Reality and Authority in the universe. This obligation entails faithfulness to a centuries-long practice of reverent attentiveness to sacred texts and disciplined community interpretation of and reflection on those texts. Stated philosophically, it involves deriving from the foundation of the community's religious classics an ontological understanding of who the Jew and Christian are and what she and he are called to contribute to the healing of God's creation (*tikkun 'olam*). As for its political impact, it is important to recognize that acknowledgement of the sole ultimate authority of God relativizes all human regimes, institutions and powers, limiting their claims on their citizens to a penultimate status, and that only to the extent that they conform to the standards of righteousness that are inherent in God's universal rule.

In my Lutheran tradition, the place where that essential identity is formed is in the presence of God in worship through the Word and the Sacraments. Accordingly, I maintain that worship constitutes the first step in a theo-political hermeneutic capable of guiding a faith community committed to living in the world as agents of God's compassionate justice. Perhaps we can best guard against the common American tendency to privatize religion while at the same time emphasizing the importance of securing the foundation before building the superstructure with this audacious assertion: Worship is the most political act in which a person of faith can engage![3]

Specification of the responsibility members of a community of faith have to the society and world understood as parts of God's domain occurs in an ensuing act of performance, one that constitutes the second step in a viable theo-political hermeneutic, namely, study, study in the church basement, in the seminary, in the retreat center, in the home, where moral issues, both personal, social, and international, are discussed in relation to the foundational classics of the community with the goal of clarifying specific policies and strategies that can be inferred from our sacred texts and from our identity as citizens of God's universal reign. This study shares with worship a communitarian character, occurring as it does within the comfort and safety of one's spiritual family where, what can become the scandal of particularity in the public square, is simply the shared language of one large family. While familial in nature, and thus inevitably parochial, such study constitutes the authentic basis for a faith community's engagement with the larger society and world, inasmuch as the specificity of its contribution is derived from the depths of its religious heritage, separated from which its particularity becomes blurred and its engagement in public discourse becomes anemic and indistinguishable from secular agencies within the larger society.[4] As we engage our fellow communicants within the context of our particular religious communities in ethical and political discourse, we are thus performing the second most political act of which the person of faith is capable, and this before we even have entered the public square!

A new challenge confronts us as we move to step three, which involves the movement from the performance of faith as an inner-community exercise to the practice of faith in the public realm. Within the context of the First Amendment tradition that is central to the discussion of religion and politics in the United States, arguments range from the categorical inappropriateness of bringing religiously based arguments into public debate to the assertion that a faith community must boldly give testimony to it beliefs and convictions without attempts to make that testimony compatible, or even comprehensible, to other ears.

Here we will limit ourselves to clarification of the distinction between the theo-political hermeneutic we adopt and two alternatives, inasmuch as we find in those alternatives a mixture of useful and unsuitable features.

Consider first the communitarianism of Stanley Hauerwas, who draws on the philosophy of Alistair Macintyre and the theology of John Yoder. Our affinities with Hauerwas relate to his emphasis on the indispensability of a religious community's fidelity to its religious heritage, without which it severs its tie to the source of its contribution to the larger society and world and divests its testimony of passion and urgency. We are in agreement with Hauerwas that both the intellectual substance and deep compassion that are requisite to the faith community's contribution to the wider world depend on its faithfulness to its biblical and confessional foundation. But a distinction must also be made: It is not sufficient for the faith community to live in obedience and give testimony to its moral principles in the untranslated categories of its heritage. As agents of a God who cares for his entire creation, it must also address a society that speaks in the tongues of myriad religions and moral philosophies in comprehensible terms suitable for inclusive, civil discourse.

This brings us to the programmatic work of John Rawls and his claim that the key to civil discourse within a religiously and philosophically diverse society is agreement on a neutral starting point, one stripped of the scandal of particularity represented by the comprehensive doctrines of specific religious and ideological communities. That starting point is a theory of justice that intentionally refrains from providing a society with a universal worldview or privileging one such view over others, accepting instead the more modest goal of providing a context for civil dialogue through the guarantee of the liberty and equal rights of all participants. We do not need to enter into the hair-splitting exercise of differentiating the early Rawls from the later, since in both, religiously grounded arguments have no autonomous status in public debate, where rational argument alone carries weight.

Though Rawls at first blush seems to provide the key for moving from the particularity of individual belief systems to the inclusiveness of public discourse, his system both strips religious communities of their freedom of giving public expression to their faith-based moral principles and privileges its own particular ideology, that of rationalism. Though purporting to uphold the First Amendment tradition, Rawls instead undermines that tradition's stringent twin-safeguards.

In seeking to conceptualize the third step of a theo-political hermeneutic that will benefit from valid insights in both Hauerwas and Rawls while avoiding the pitfalls in each, I find myself attracted to the thought of Jeffrey Stout[5] and in agreement with the theological reflections of David Novak. Inherent in biblical tradition, in both its Jewish and Christian iterations, is an intricate understanding of reality that is predicated on faithfulness to the ultimate beliefs and loyalties of one's particular community that at the same time includes affirmation of the integrity and equal rights of all the families in God's vast creation. Though Scripture contains strands that can be elicited as warrants for theological exclusivism and its attendant disparagement of all who differ, the Judaism of Novak and the Christianity with which I identify provide the foundation for a political theory well suited for a democratic society. Since any human government belongs not to the category of the ultimate universal rule belonging alone to God but to the penultimate realm of human society, all communities, whether religious, agnostic, or atheist, are welcomed participants. Especially in relation to other religious communities, what the Christian and Jew desires is participation benefiting from the same in-depth connection with foundational sources that is viewed as essential to their own identity and hence potential contribution to the commonweal.

What we are describing is a cultural maturity transcending tolerance and respect for human rights based on social contract. We speak of inalienable human rights derived not merely from human good will but from the infinite wisdom of the Ruler of all peoples. The model of government that ensues is not one based on principles determined by human savants, but on principles that have been in place from the creation of the universe. Human governments are not extrapolations from the ideal categories of a particular school of philosophy, but are temporal constructions negotiated by all of the participating individuals and groups who are engaged in the civil process of reaching agreed-upon goals via the most effective and fair policies and strategies imaginable, which constructions remain open to critique and revision.

Inclusive, civil discourse in which all participants are encouraged to draw upon the particularities of their own religious and moral traditions is what I designate as stage four of my theo-political hermeneutic. It stands in dialectical relation to stage two, because from the give and take of public discourse Jews and Christians return to the safety of their own communities having been chastened, edified, and challenged by encounter with citizens whose political positions have been shaped by traditions differing from their own, citizens viewed not as opponents but as provocateurs, and, in the case of Jews and Christians, cousins charged with distinct but ultimately related purposes in God's redemptive plan for creation.

Here we offer one example of how the explicit beliefs and moral principles of Jews and Christians can enter into public debate in such a manner as neither to compromise the particularity of their belief systems nor transgress the limits imposed on religion and state by the First Amendment. A subject of intense debate in the public realm is the question of whether it is the responsibility of democratic societies to guarantee the rights of its citizens and to advocate for international human rights on the basis of a negative or a positive definition of rights. Classically in social contract theory, rights are defined in negative terms, that is, the human is entitled to exercise his or her freedom up to the point where the rights of another are violated. The Universal Declaration of Human Rights produced by the United Nations Human Rights Commission formulated a much more comprehensive definition of human rights, namely, the rights of all people to the benefits of nutrition, security, healthcare, etc., that optimize their full potential as human beings. Within Judaism and Christianity moral principles have developed over the centuries that emphatically support the positive definition, principles stemming from a particular understanding of God's nature and God's relation to humans as manifested in paradigmatic events like the Exodus and revealed in the Torah of Moses and the Beatitudes of Jesus. In entering into the public debate regarding human rights with substantive arguments and moral convictions rooted in their sacred traditions, Jews and Christians remain loyal to religious beliefs and moral principles derived from their particular historical ontologies at the same as they abide by the rules for debate appropriate for a multi-cultural, religiously diverse society.

Finally I come to stage five, which stands as a bookend complementing the act of worship of stage one. If worship is the most political thing the person of faith can do, inasmuch as it is the lifeline securing her historical-ontological identity as a child of God in the world for the sake of the world, then stage five, the blessed vision of the fulfillment of God's creative purpose in the messianic redemption (*ge'ulah*), is the most sublime thing the person of faith can possess, enabling her to hear the whispers of angels and glimpse the very Glory of the Most High. The blessed vision of the *eschton* is a special gift of God to his children that the secular world, with its reduction of reality to a material universe, tries its utmost to obliterate.[6] What is more, the political significance of that vision of eschatological fulfillment should not be overlooked, for in it is contained assurance that when participation in programs of justice and reform is obstructed by opposing forces, when the ridicule of cultural despisers of religion reaches its highest pitch, when the wicked prosper and the righteous suffer, even then hope in final redemption is not lost. In that vision is also contained a safeguard against the temptation on the reverse side of despair, namely, the flush of human pride over accomplishments and perceptions of social progress that lead to a secularization of teleology and an impoverishment of theological imagination.[7] In times of defeat as in times of victory, the one whose vision remains focused on God's ineffable goal of universal *shalom* will neither despair nor exult, but will give God alone the glory and be satisfied to enter night's rest with a prayer of thanks for being able to be a faithful servant of the King of the Universe.[8]

Where Jews and Christians differ
Though the theo-political hermeneutic we have been describing provides a context within which all religious groups and ethical associations can join in building the good society, we rejoice in the fact that a special relationship exists between Jews and Christians. Setting aside the obvious facts that broad diversity exists *within* these two religions and that certain affinities are felt more strongly across the two groups than within, we would be avoiding an essential part of our topic were we not to speak for a moment of the different interpretations of Scripture that distinguish Judaism and Christianity as two distinct religions. At the center of this discussion are topics such as Eretz Yisrael, ritual law, and the figure of Jesus Christ, variously understood among students of the Bible as errant teacher, Cynic philosopher, apocalyptic seer, or Messiah.

Substantive discussions between believing Jews and Christians are essential on several levels. No starker reminder of this fact could be imagined than the Shoah. Repentance motivating ongoing study of the roots of Christian anti-Judaism, self-examination of persisting sources of misrepresentation and prejudice within the Church, and a genuine hunger to continue an exercise that remains in its infancy stage, namely, the exercise of learning from the vast knowledge and wisdom of Judaism, all of these are contributions that Judaism continues to make to Christianity. And of course our present topic emphasizes the need that we have for each other's insights into the attrition being experienced within our communities and the challenges we face as we seek to relate the treasures of our tradition to a society and world in need.

One of the unfinished tasks in Jewish-Christian relations is conversation aimed at more adequate understandings of the historical Jewish figure, Jesus of Nazareth, including his relation to the tradition of biblical prophecy, his eschatology, his approach to interpreting Mosaic Torah, and his strategy for dealing with contemporary Jewish parties as well as the temple hierarchy, the Herodians, and the Roman occupation. I have organized some of my thoughts on this topic in a publication that will appear in 2009 and thus limit myself here to this passing reference.[9]

Having acknowledged dimensions of the distinctiveness of our two religions, I wish to close by drawing attention to shared beliefs and longings that transcend differences and reaffirm our ultimate covenantal bond. I look to one passage from Isaiah and another from the Apostle Paul that enrich my vision of the eschaton as the sublime culmination of the religious and political vocations of all who love and fear the Creator of the Universe, among whom we are blessed to be included.

In Isaiah 2:2-4 the prophet invites us to rejoice in God's restoration of Zion, to which the nations are drawn by the irresistible lure of Torah, the study of which leads them to recast their weapons of destruction into implements of peace and shared prosperity.

In Romans 8 the Apostle looks with hope beyond suffering and futility to the day of the Lord when "the creation itself will be set free from its bondage to decay and will obtain the freedom of the glory of the children of God" (v. 21).

In sharing such glimpses of God's completion of the plan for which the universe and all its creatures were called into being, we as Jews and Christians find the solid foundation for our work together. We have not arrived at that final scene, and we live without timetables and astronomical signs, but what we do possess is a hope predicated on our faith that the God who has brought us this far is the one in whose hands the future—including the final future—lies, and on our confidence that the path into that future is one that will bring us ever closer together.

Paul of Tarsus may have complicated things in many ways for circles of Jews and Christians seeking to understand what unites and what divides them, but it is he who may have taught Christians their most important theological lesson, and with it I shall end:

"When all things are subjected to God, then the Son himself will also be subjected to the one who put all things in subjection under him, so that God may be all in all" (I Cor 15:28).

Notes

1. Novak, David, *The Jewish Social Contract: An Essay in Political Theology* (Princeton, NJ: Princeton University Press, 2005).
2. Huntington, Samuel P., *The Clash of Civilizations and the Remaking of World Order* (New York: Touchstone, 1997).
3. For a more detailed description of the role of worship in a theo-political hermeneutic, see "Restoring a Moral Compass for Navigating a Precarious World," in Biblical Imagination: Scripture and the Life of Faith: Essays in Honor of Christopher Bryan (Sewanee Theological Review 50:1 [2006]) 32-50.
4. My understanding of the vital importance of rootedness in the specific stories and performances of one's faith community is indebted to the unflinching prophetic witness of Stanley Hauerwas, though as shall be seen immediately below, I believe that communitarianism, while essential to the preservation of authentic religious testimonies in a pluralistic society, is inadequate as a vehicle for translating the significance of those testimonies into public discourse. See Hauerwas, Stanley, *Performing the Faith: Bonhoeffer and the Practice of Nonviolence* (Grand Rapids, MI: Brazos Press, 2004).
5. Stout, Jeffrey, *Democracy and Tradition* (Princeton, NJ: Princeton University Press, 2004).
6. How sad it is to witness the large number of children raised in Jewish and Christian families who under the influence of a secular/materialist worldview reduce their vision of reality to Freud's construal of life as circumscribed by sex and death!
7. As has often been observed, this temptation derailed the Social Gospel movement of the last decades of the nineteenth century and the opening decade of the twentieth, leading to Karl Barth's scathing critique and the emergence of neo-orthodoxy.
8. Useful as primers in the patience of an eschatological faith are Jeremiah's word to Baruch in Jeremiah 45 and Jesus' saying about the slave returned from his day's labor in Luke 17:7-10.
9. Hanson, P. D., "We Once Knew Him from a Human Point of View", in A. Schuele and G. Thomas (eds.), *Who Is Jesus Christ for Us Today? Pathways to Contemporary Christology* (Louisville KY: Westminster John Knox Press, 2009), pp. 203–218.

DEMOCRATIC STRUCTURES AND DEMOCRATIC CULTURES
A "Response" to Paul Hanson and David Novak

Mark Douglas

Paul Hanson and David Novak raise arguments both helpful and profound in thinking about the changing complexities of religious voices speaking in the public sphere.[1] Thinking as I do that Hanson and Novak get things basically right—that religious voices speak not from nowhere but from particular religious traditions; that though those voices have played an important role in U.S. history, the forces of cultural secularism over the last half century tended to restrict their speech in the public sphere; that those forces are in retreat and religious voices are getting a greater hearing in that sphere; and that these changes ought to drive religious voices not primarily toward celebration but toward critical, charitable, responsible, and (above all) particularistic engagement with the public sphere—I do not intend to rehearse Hanson and Novak's respective arguments here. Instead, I want to take up the challenges they have laid before us to think as a Christian who is in conversation with Jews about both why and how Christians should be interested in the public sphere.

The focal point for both Novak and Hanson is the structures of the democratic systems that make an active public square both viable and necessary. Almost 175 years ago, Alexis De Tocqueville highlighted the importance of broad public engagement on political matters in making the American democratic experiment work. Assuming that Tocqueville's claims in *Democracy in America*[2] still pertain, it would follow (at least to the extent that they believe in the benefits of such a democratic experiment) that Christians, Jews, and other citizens ought properly be interested in two sets of questions toward shaping a sustainable public square. The first of questions has to do with the structures of the public square and their relation to democratic governance. Such questions include at least the following: Who gets to speak? What language(s) are allowed or prohibited? With whom should we speak? Who should be listening? And how should the listeners carry their discoveries back into their various projects of governing faithfully, gathering privately, and growing individually? It is these questions, especially, that Hanson, Novak, and a host of other religious and non-religious political philosophers have so helpfully pursued of late.

The second set of questions overlaps the first but has less to do with structural matters than with cultural ones. This set includes questions like: Why should we be interested in speaking or listening? What are the benefits and burdens (to us, to our families and communities, to civil society, to government, etc.) of maintaining a vital public square? What are the cultural resources that sustain such a space, what cultural programs and movements harm it, and what is the relation between those resources and programs? And how deep ought our various commitments to the public square be in light of other commitments that we may hold more dearly? If the first set of questions is pursued by political philosophers and magistrates (from John Locke to John Rawls, from the local constabulary to the Supreme Court), the latter are more the domain of public intellectuals and poets (Cornell West and Walt Whitman, Bill Bennett and the editors of *The New York Times*).

Hanson and Novak remind us that the answers to the first set of questions will be particular to the idiomatic understandings of the various communities of faith pursuing them. Taking my cue from them, I want to explore answers to the second set of questions—but, again, in light of various idiomatic claims and commitments that arise out of particular communities of faith. Or, to restate that a bit more clearly: I want to inquire into reasons that (Reformed) Christians and Jews should be interested in engaging in conversations in the public square as those reasons arise out of the two faith traditions. But first, a bit of background and a few observations.

Faith, culture, and the public square: a rehearsal and the problems of not rehearsing

That matters of faith influence politics and culture is unsurprising. In the United States, they have always done so. From the arrival of Pilgrims, Puritans, and Quakers before the country's founding to the continued influence of churches, synagogues, and other houses of worship on laws, on candidates, on social welfare, and even on leisure time, religion and culture have always been inextricably and potently mixed.

This influence has had many benefits: promoting social stability, maintaining traditions of volunteerism and altruism, shaping political language and enriching culture. Yet it hasn't been only beneficial. Religion, after all, has a long history of promoting division, rejecting wisdom, and exacerbating violence. Anyone who would speak religiously in the public sphere has the obligation of recognizing not only religion's benefits but its costs as well.

Indeed, attention to the dangers associated with religion's costs helped shape the United States' traditions of secularism: political secularism, which, via the First Amendment, maintains a separation of church and state, and cultural secularism, which has sought to emphasize the distinction between public and private (and to place religion in the private realm) as a way of culturally undergirding political secularism. Collectively, the effect of these two traditions of secularism has been an attempt to keep religious voices not only out of government but out of the public sphere as well (or, at very most, to insist that religious people translate their religious language into one that could be understood by everyone.) A history of religious perspectives given public expression in the U.S. (e.g., during abolition and the civil rights movement) did little to shape the opinions of many secular philosophers that religion was quaint at best, for the weak-minded in general and the cause of atrocities on occasion. Given its potentially divisive impact, even the generously minded tended to treat religion like strong medicine: to be administered only as needed and in small doses. Such were the arguments of secularism, anyway.

For quite a while it looked like the cultural secularist argument was winning. Religious folk tended to respond either in reactionary ways or in agreement with secularism. They allowed the promoters of secularism to shape the argument; as a result even when religious folk won particular battles (e.g., keeping a moment of silence in public schools, getting government vouchers for private schools), it still looked like they were fighting a rear-guard action. In spite of the fact that fears of godlessness in American society had been around almost as long as there was such a place as America,[3] during the 1960s and 1970s it seemed that the forces of history were moving conclusively toward the victory of secularization and the dissolution of publicly valued religious authority in the west.

It's not that there was no religious language in public settings but that where religious language was being used—like printing "In God We Trust" on money and adding "under God" to the pledge of allegiance—it tended to be pretty innocuous language. It was a kind of "here's something we all agree on" approach that denied the actual disagreements that particular people of faith might have with each other and thereby significantly circumscribed the "we" who were agreeing—a kind of common denominator approach to religious sentiment that revealed itself via the rather peculiar argument-at least to many active Christians and Jews—that there was such a thing as "The Judeo-Christian Ethic."

Indeed, one way to think about this kind of common denominator faith is as the residue that remains after all the rich but clearly distinct religious languages have been pulverized and screened by the secularist project: it's what a universally shared (and therefore publicly accessible) faith language would sound like if such a thing could actually exist; a way of avoiding the perceived social costs that come with religious pluralism by denying pluralism a foothold in the public sphere.

However, there is no universally shared faith language. Instead, as the variety of religions in the U.S. increased and the frustrations of people with particular religious perspectives grew, the arguments for secularization began to be drowned out by the cacophony of new and very particular religious voices, each claiming the right to speak in their native tongues.

Before such an onslaught, it was almost inevitable that secularization would lose. And it did. Its chief proponents (e.g., Rawls) either died or changed their minds.[4] Sympathetic political philosophers and theologians pointed to the double standard used to privatize religious perspectives while allowing various ideological perspectives into the increasingly pluralistic public sphere.[5] Historians paid more attention to the benefits of religious voices in that sphere. Religious conservatives for whom secularization was a dirty word gained political power. An ascendant

Republican Party threw their weight behind the project of establishing government grants for faith-based initiatives. Immigrant groups coming from non-secular states grew in number even as secular citizens in the west became more globalized and noticed the impact of religion to shape politics in, for example, Iran or Poland. And people everywhere in the U.S. looked around and noticed not only how religious the culture was but how frequently many of its citizens were willing to listen to religious perspectives at least in the name of tolerance. Cultural secularity—or at least the arguments that undergirded it—fell out of style. Not everyone is happy about it, but for all intents and purposes, we now live in a post-secular world.

So now it is (mostly) settled that faith matters in the public square—that religious thinkers neither have to leave their faith at the door when they enter the square nor translate their religious perspectives into a shared secular vernacular. There is common consent *that* faith matters in such a setting. But *why* and *how* faith matters is far less clear—and religious folk have done little to settle those questions.

By the time we were given permission to speak in our own idiomatic tongues, people of faith seemed to have forgotten how to talk in ways that were both faithful and publicly meaningful. Perhaps this is because we have been affected by the same trends that helped us gain admission into the public square (e.g., growing pluralism, the retrenchment of religion in and against society, the growing political power of religious conservatives, greater attention to the way earlier generations of religious voices had spoken). Perhaps we had internalized the public/private split that marks secularization and had decided the most important matters we could talk about were internal ones (like whether or not to ordain gays and lesbians). Perhaps some of us entered the public square looking for a fight against secularists rather than seeking a new way to speak and be heard. And, as people so often do, perhaps we cut intellectual corners and tried to say simply things that are, by nature complicated (much as the last few paragraphs did, having taken a complex set of arguments and boiled them down into a few broad stereotypes). Having spent so little time rehearsing our lines, we were affected by the political equivalent of stage fright once we were allowed to speak in the public square—and so we did the same things most frightened performers do: mumbled, got angry, or repeated earlier lines.

The mumblers continued the project of shaping a common denominator faith, albeit one that is oriented more toward personal transformation than social stability. Religious language could be public language provided it spoke to everyone's situation, albeit in vague and aphoristic ways (a friend calls this "therapeutic deism"). Religious faith became faith in one's own project of self-fulfillment and religious language became the language of diffused spirituality (as in "I'm spiritual but not religious"). Where a common faith used to help maintain social stability, now it served the ends of personal growth; advancing projects of individual spiritual growth and personal wellbeing replaced those of communal growth and public welfare as the chief purposes of religious activity.

At least from the perspective of a thriving public sphere, the sooner such an approach disappears, the better. The fear that discrepant religious languages would disrupt the robust conversations necessary for a thriving public sphere led to the development of an approach to religion that treated the public sphere principally as the location in which to share the pleasures of private spirituality. But it is almost certain that such an approach, which does little beyond preaching tolerance for diversity, fails to fuel those robust conversations. Tolerance and diversity are important, but they only become meaningful when we take seriously the perspectives of those who disagree with us, and common denominator spirituality has been shaped to reject those very disagreements. Lacking either the motivation or the procedures necessary to address significant public differences, the spiritual-but-not-religious types retreat to their private spaces, unable to work up interest in much-needed public conversations. Ironically, the secular project has helped to bring about the very thing it feared: a diminished public sphere—though diminished not through uncontrolled antagonism but by personal apathy. Initially unwilling to be public without being religious, some religious folk discovered a way to be religious without being really public.

The angry attempted to overcome the diversity of religious voices in that sphere by controlling it. The attacks have been two-pronged. One prong has accepted a vision of the world in which the state is the dominant player in politics and politics the dominant force in culture; they've attempted to foist their candidates upon the rest of us, to position themselves as close to the sources of political power as possible, and to speak as loudly as they can not so much in the public square as toward the halls of power. The other prong has recognized the degree to which culture precedes politics; they've attempted to make themselves arbiters of what is good or right in culture, to aggressively market their own products, and to co-opt the languages of other groups to their own purposes (e.g., "right to life" from the right and "freedom to marry" from the left—though they leave unclear how the languages of rights and freedoms fit Christian visions of why we care for others or how we understand covenantal commitments).

The effect of such an approach hasn't been to make the public sphere monolithic but to make it more contentious. It hasn't overcome a pluralistic culture so much as exacerbated divisions within culture. No wonder many people are uninterested in engaging in the conversations of the public square; they fear they're likely only to be yelled at. The very danger that most pre-occupied those pursuing the secularist project came to pass—ironically, though, because attempting to keep religious voices silent in the public sphere meant religious people were poorly prepared in speaking both faithfully and lovingly once they entered it.

The line-repeaters seem to have ignored the demise of cultural secularism. Having grown used to translating the language of their faith commitments into the vernacular of the public sphere, they carried on as if that vernacular were their native language. They regularly make statements about the various economic, political, and social afflictions of the day—but always making those statements in largely non-religious terms. In part, their approach was shaped by practical considerations: they regularly form coalitions with politically and socially similar groups from non-religious coalitions or other religious traditions and the secular language of the public sphere has been helpful in keeping those coalitions focused on their objectives rather than on their constituent members. Where Jews and Christians have worked together to affect social change, this has usually been their approach—partly so they didn't bog down in confusion about each others' speech and partly because they didn't want the broader public to trip over their language on the way to garnering that public's assent.

These were tactical considerations and, in themselves, unproblematic. The danger with such an approach arose when these Christians and Jews returned to their churches and synagogues and had trouble connecting the public vernacular that had grown comfortable on their tongues to the idiomatic languages of the faith. Successful at being public, they struggled at being a church or synagogue.

This approach to the use (or, more properly, non-use) of religious language in the public square may not have been especially helpful to believers but it hasn't done any immediate damage to that square. And many important social programs have been nourished by the socially active tendencies of many who took this approach. But it is an open question as to whether this approach can actually nourish Constitutional democracy over the long run. If everyone expresses their commitments—faith and otherwise—by first translating them into a common language, where are the advantages that come with hearing different perspectives likely to come from?

These three different approaches to using religious language in a post-secular public sphere—mumbling, getting angry, and repeating earlier lines—share at least two common tendencies. The first is that none of these approaches is especially informed by the theological commitments of their respective faiths. Giving a pass to questions about how faith might matter in the public sphere, they risk draining public discourse of the possibilities that might follow from the admission of faith-language into that discourse. Not asking *how* faith matters, they diminish the profundity of the recognition *that* faith matters.[6] And, second, they share a pre-occupation with the problems of religious pluralism. The first approach seeks a religious approach that need not be pluralistic; the second seeks to overcome pluralism with a particular religious perspective; the third succumbs to the fears about pluralism that drove the secularist project in the first place.

But what if we treated religious pluralism neither a threat (as secularism and the religious agreement-by-domination perspective make it out to be) nor an epiphenomenal mask that hides a common faith (as the religion-as-therapy perspective makes it out to be)? What if we treated pluralism like we treat religious particularity: simply as a fact of life—a sign that people not only don't think alike when it comes to religious faith but that their commitments to those various faiths will inevitably shape their interactions with each other? What if the inevitable concerns that come with admitting many religious perspectives into the public sphere aren't so much problems to be resolved as conditions to be lived with, keeping in mind that the alternatives to living with those concerns (confusion, coercion, cooption) are worse?

"Faithful" reasons for engaging in the public square

If pluralism and particularity are simply conditions to be lived with, it would follow that particular types of Christians and Jews—which is to say, all of them—have twin obligations: to accept the fact that it is within neither their ability nor their purview to overcome pluralism and to give arguments about why the public square—in all its pluralism—matters to them on the basis of their particular understandings of God, the world, and the public square. In what follows, I highlight five possible bases for Christians and Jews to think of engagement in the public square as an important part of their particular faith commitments.

1. Biblical authenticity

Almost from the creation stories at the beginning of Genesis there has been a repeated refrain that runs through the scriptures. It is this: faith has implications for how to live with others. Whether focused on matters of justice (Moses before Pharaoh, the warnings and promises of the Old Testament prophets, Jesus' command to care for the "least of these"), righteousness (Abraham's hospitality to angelic visitors, Job's dealings with his so-called "comforters," Paul's call submit to secular authorities), or witness (Israel's call to be a blessing to the nations, Jesus delivering the Sermon on the Mount to the gathered crowds, Peter preaching in the marketplace), the refrain is clear: the Bible does not support a "just God and me" faith.

2. Historical precedent

In the long histories of church and synagogue, they have always been most relevant when facing outward. Sometimes that relevance has been less-than-laudatory: scandals like the Crusades, missionary endeavors less interested in sharing the gospel than in obliterating indigenous cultures for their own advantages, Zionist pre-tensions toward claiming more land and refusing to live with Palestinians, and, above all, the *Shoah*, perpetrated by a particular group of Christians claiming to know the mind of God on matters of race and salvation. But both church and synagogue have also shaped profound—and profoundly good—movements in history. They have established countless charitable organizations, hospitals, and support services. They've led fights against slavery, segregation, apartheid, and totalitarian governments. They've built schools, led literacy movements, and run after-school programs. They've dug wells, built houses and worked to make them homes. They've lobbied for more just laws and on behalf of the under- or unrepresented. One would be hard pressed to find any part of the globe that they have not touched and, in touching it, done good works.

3. Doxological commitment

Believing that God is the primary audience for all their actions, Christians and Jews practice at incorporating worship into more and more of their lives. They struggle *against* making too much sense of a world that can be neatly divided between matters that are "public" and matters that are "private." In a way, they recognize that everything they do has a public: the God whom they seek to glorify in their actions. Obviously, this doesn't mean that they can't understand or value actions that ought to be protected from interference by others in the community or the state. As Novak reminds us, at a political level, Christians and Jews see the importance of preserving and maintaining such space. But at an existential level, Christians and Jews live their lives before God and, as such, properly ought to refuse to let the distinction between public and private go all the way down. The worship—praise, confession, thanksgiving, supplication—that shapes their whole lives will necessarily occur both in politically public and politically private spaces and thereby undermine claims that put too much emphasis on keeping public and private apart.

4. Theological credibility

Christians and Jews cannot make sense of their faiths without seeing the world as a sphere of divine activity nor make sense of themselves without trying to discern how God's activity in the world is both shaping and encouraging their actions in it. Whether through the practices of Torah maintenance or claims about the continued presence of the Holy Spirit, Jews and Christians recognize that God's interactions with the world extend beyond their borders. Churches and synagogues face outward—including toward the public square—because they believe they can seek God there as well.

5. Moral responsibility

Both Christians and Jews treat the commandment regarding neighbor-love as near the core of their moral commitments.[7] Those neighbors are not us; nor, necessarily, are they like us. They will have different faiths, different worldviews, different opinions, and different values. Undoubtedly, contact with those differences will create tensions. But at the same time, it will also put Jews and Christians in places where they can see a new revelation or hear a fresh word from the God who is at work in the world, often through those very neighbors.[8]

No doubt it is clear that the way any particular expression of Judaism or Christianity picks up one or more of these justifications for engagement in the public sphere will be shaped by the way that expression understands scripture, tradition, worship, theology, and ethics and their relationship to each other as well as the different values, virtues, and doctrines that each group idiomatically exercises. I recognize that the collection of five reasons I've given above functions as an overview and, therefore, a set of generalizations. It is not intended to suggest that all Jews and all Christians share something in common and that what they share should be the basis for a general Judeo-Christian ethic. Each of the reasons above is malleable, constantly being shaped in very particular ways according to the theological emphases of particular religious communities. Indeed, I've only just begun to name differences between Jewish and Christian approaches to these matters; far more explication could still be done. Moreover, I imagine that the differences between such religious groups will make for some uncomfortable times. But such will always be the case in a pluralistic public square.

I hope, though, that it is also clear that regardless of the way that particular faith communities approach the public square in light of these reasons, they at least have the advantage of arising out of Jewish and Christian visions of the world rather than being imposed on those visions from the outside and then justified by being covered by a thin religious veneer. They are at least more congruent to the internal perspectives of faith communities than the various secular arguments for such engagement (e.g., that one has a right to carry faith into the public sphere, that robust and diverse conversations in the public sphere make it—and therefore society—stronger, that leaving the system will let others dictate morality and public purpose for society, etc.), especially now that religious individuals don't need to advance secular arguments in order to be taken seriously in the public square anyway.

Finally, I hope it is clear that the point of these arguments isn't to provide a theological justification for the structure of the public sphere. For the purposes of this reflection, at least, I have left such justifications to Novak, Hanson, and others. Instead, the point of these arguments is to accessibly name broad reasons for Christians and Jews to actually get involved in the public square as particular kinds of Christians and particular kinds of Jews. It is to stimulate a culture of civic engagement not because Jews and Christians are primarily interested in promoting civic engagement but because they can't make sense of how to live in all their particularity as Christians and Jews without doing so.

Notes

Portions of this response are taken from a book manuscript currently under review.

1. Hanson's article is available in this issue of *Cross Currents*. For Novak's thoughts, see his *The Jewish Social Contract: An Essay in Political Theology* (Princeton, NJ: Princeton University Press, 2005), esp. Chapter 1.

2. de Tocqueville, Alexis, *Democracy in America*, ed. by Isaac Kramnick, trans. by Gerald Bevan (New York: Penguin Classics, 2003).

3. See, e.g., Mathewes, Charles, and Christopher McKnight Nichols, eds., *Prophecies of Godlessness: Predictions of America's Imminent Secularization from the Puritans to the Present Day* (New York: Oxford UP, 2008).

4. It's worth noting—and exploring further, though not here—that John Rawls, Jurgen Habermas, and Jacque Derrida (who are arguably the premier philosophers of their age in each of their respective countries) all revised their work to better incorporate religious perspectives in the public square. Maybe it's worth also musing on the fact that each did so near the end of his life, but definitely not here.

5. Here I would give special commendation to the work of Nicholas Wolterstorff, including *Religion in the Public Square: The Place of Religious Convictions in Political Debate* (Lanham, MD: Rowman and Littlefield, 1996).

6. Leading, almost inevitably, toward the ascendance of theological suspicions *a la* Stanley Hauerwas that Christians (and, to a lesser extent, Jews) should even get involved in public matters or civic activities. See, for example, the new book, *Electing Not to Vote: Christian Reflections on Reasons for Not Voting*, ed. by Ted Lewis (Brockton, MA: Cascade Books, 2008).

7. I have elsewhere argued that for Christians, at least, Jews are among our closest neighbors (historically, theologically, and, in much of the world, geographically) and as such, the command to love our neighbors ought always catch Christians up in questions about how

to shape their relationships with Jewish communities. And given both a history in which many Christians have either persecuted Jews or stood by and allowed those persecutions to happen and also the recognition that Judaism has significantly fewer adherents than any other major religion, it may behoove Christians to pay close attention to the situations in which their Jewish brothers and sisters find themselves, especially where they live as small minorities within larger populations.

8. It occurs to me that there is at least one additional reason that Christians might for engaging in the public square. Unlike Judaism in which usually one is Jewish because one's parents are (or the eastern religions which claim that everyone participates in the cycle of birth and reincarnation whether they follow the teachings of those faiths in any particular incarnation or not), the Christian faith has consistently held that becoming a Christian is a matter of conversion or transformation, not natural processes. One becomes Christian by rebirth; not by birth. Even children do not fully become members of the church until they can willingly make their own faith statements. As such, the church faces toward the world—at least in part—because that is where it finds its new members. This reason creates any number of tensions between Christianity and other religions (and, at least in the United States, particularly between Christianity and Judaism of late). That tension may be slightly mitigated by the recognition that Judaism also allows for conversion to the faith, but my suspicion is that this tension—like all tensions between groups in the public square—is something to be lived with and shaped by the structures that form the public square rather than something to be resolved or eliminated from that square.

CONTRIBUTORS

P. Mark Achtemeier is Associate Professor of Systematic Theology at the University of Dubuque Theological Seminary. He is the author with Andrew Purves of *Union in Christ: A Declaration for the Church*, and *A Passion for the Gospel: Confessing Jesus Christ for the 21st Century*.

Samuel E. Balentine is Professor of Old Testament at Union Theological Seminary and Presbyterian School of Education. He is the author of four books, including a commentary on Leviticus in the Interpretation Bible Commentary series (Westminster John Knox Press) and *The Torah's Vision of Worship* (Fortress Press, 1999).

Nina Beth Cardin is the General Consultant for COEJL and Director of the Baltimore Jewish Environmental Network (BJEN) at the Pearlstone Conference and Retreat Center, which is dedicated to promoting environmental advocacy, ethics, and behavior. She is immediate past Director of Jewish Life at the JCC of Greater Baltimore.

Rosann M. Catalano is the Associate Director of the Institute for Christian & Jewish Studies as well as the ICJS's Roman Catholic Scholar.

Andrew Foster Connors is the pastor of Brown Memorial Park Avenue Presbyterian Church in Baltimore.

Mark Douglas is Associate Professor of Christian Ethics at Columbia Theological Seminary. He is the author of *Confessing Christ in the 21st Century*.

Adam Gregerman is Jewish Scholar at the Institute for Christian-Jewish Studies in Baltimore. Dr. Gregerman's main academic area is Ancient Judaism, though he focuses on the complex relationship between both Judaism and Christianity from antiquity through the present.

Paul D. Hanson is Florence Corliss Lamont Professor of Divinity at Harvard Divinity School. The author of many books, Professor Hanson is currently working to complete a book examining the interplay between religion and politics, with emphasis on American faith communities rooted in biblical tradition.

Christopher M. Leighton is an ordained Presbyterian minister who has served as the Executive Director of the Institute for Christian & Jewish Studies in Baltimore since its inception in 1987.

Douglas F. Ottati is the Craig Family Distinguished Professor in Reformed Theology and Justice Ministry. He is co-general editor of the multi-volume series, *The Library of Theological Ethics*. Recent books include *Theology for Liberal Presbyterians and Other Endangered Species*,

Reforming Protestantism: Christian Commitment in Today's World, and *Hopeful Realism: Recovering the Poetry of Theology.*

John T. Pawlikowski is Professor of Ethics and Director of the Catholic-Jewish Studies Program at Catholic Theological Union. He is president of the International Council of Christians and Jews and author of *Christ in the Light of the Christian Jewish Dialogue* and co-editor with Judith Banki of *Ethics in the Shadow of the Holocaust.*

William Plevan is a Ph.D. candidate in the Department of Religion at Princeton University, which he entered after earning his rabbinic ordination from the Jewish Theological Seminary. He is currently working on his dissertation, entitled: "I, Thou, We: Martin Buber's Philosophical Anthropology Reconsidered."

Randi Rashkover is Director of Jewish Studies at George Mason University and a contributing editor of *Cross-Currents*. Currently, she is working on a book titled *Freedom and Law: A Jewish-Christian Apologetics*.

Karen Marie Yust is Associate Professor of Christian Education at Union Theological Seminary and Presbyterian School of Education in Richmond, Virginia. Her latest book, *Taught by God*, explores the relationship between transformational learning theories and classical spiritual practices.

www.ingramcontent.com/pod-product-compliance
Lightning Source LLC
Chambersburg PA
CBHW040259170426
43193CB00020B/2946